The Students' Historical Geography of the Holy Land

THE REV. WILLIAM WALTER SMITH

A.B., A.M., M.D.

Other Works by

The Rev. WILLIAM WALTER SMITH,

A.B., A.M., M.D.

For Pupils

The Meaning of Words in the Catechism.
12 pp. Paper, 2 cents net.

The Step Catechism.
In short divisions, with meaning of words and certificate. 3 cents.

Lessons on the Life of Christ, Our Hero-King.
From the Prayer Book Gospels. A course of 33 Lessons, all pedagogical Source-Method, adaptable to Junior, Intermediate, and Senior Grades, familiarizing with use of Prayer Book and Church Year, Uniform Lesson Idea, Illustrated with a Picture for each lesson, requiring No Bibles or Testaments. 12 cents.

The Doctrines of the Church.
(40 lessons.) Seventh Edition. For Scholars of the Confirmation Age to Bible Class Requirements. 180 pp. Paper, 20 cents net; cloth, 60 cents net.

The History and Use of the Prayer Book.
(15 lessons.) Fifth Edition. For Scholars from 10 to 16. 85 pp. Paper, 16 cents net; cloth, 25 cents net.

For Teachers

The Ageless Hymns of the Living Church.
A course of 20 lessons on the sweet stories of sacred songs and their singers. Designed for the adolescent period of from 14-20 years of age. Beautifully illustrated. 120 pp. Price, 20 cents net.

Student's Historical Geography of Palestine.
65 pp. with maps. Cloth, $1.50 net.

Complete Sunday School Atlas.
32 Historical Maps in 12 colors. Paper, 35 cents net.

The Making of the Bible.
(15 lessons.) Fourth Edition. For Scholars from 11 to Adult Age. 90 pp. Paper, 12 cents net; cloth, 22 cents net.

Elements of Child Study.
A training Manual for Teachers and Normal Pupils. 277 pp. Illustrated. Cloth $1.00 net.

Religious Education.
A comprehensive Text Book. 525 pp. Cloth. Illustrated. $2.00 net.

The Sunday School of Today.
The Guide-Book for Officers and Teachers. 230 pp. Cloth Illustrated. $1.50 net.

Five-Minute Talks to Young People.
An Outline Guide for Addresses by Superintendent or Clergy. 40 pp. Cloth, 50 cents net.

Order through the New York Sunday School Commission, Inc., 416 Lafayette Street, N. Y.

The Students' Historical Geography of the Holy Land

A POPULAR READING MANUAL AND TEXT BOOK FOR
TEACHERS AND CLERGY. AN ILLUMINATING
COURSE OF LESSONS FOR THE SUNDAY
SCHOOL, TO BE USED IN THE HIS-
TORY AND GEOGRAPHY AGES

BY

THE REV. WILLIAM WALTER SMITH
A.B., A.M., M.D.

Formerly Corresponding Secretary of the Sunday School Federation,
Secretary of the New York Sunday School Commission, Inc., Sec-
retary of the New York Sunday School Association, Member of the
General Board of Religious Education, Member of the Executive
Committee and of the Teacher Training Committee of the New
York City Sunday School Association, etc.

With a Foreword by
THE REV. MILTON S. LITTLEFIELD

ILLUSTRATED WITH ONE HUNDRED HALFTONE PICTURES
OF BIBLE PLACES AND FORTY-ONE MAPS,
MOST OF THEM IN COLORS

NEW YORK
GEORGE H. DORAN COMPANY

FOREWORD

God's revelation is given to the world in three chapters. The first is the story of the land of Palestine. The second is the history of the men who made the land their home. The third is the message which the seers of Israel gave to the world.

The background of the message of the Bible is the unfolding providence of God expressed in the development of the political and religious ideas of God's people of Israel. We must know how they lived and with whom, what they did and what they thought. The background of the history is the geographical setting which made the history what it was. The story of the Hebrews is the romance of history, and Israel's place in the world has been determined in no small degree by her place on the world.

Geography and history are vitally connected. The study of the one must be interwoven with the study of the other. Geography, apart from history, is abstract and uninteresting. History, apart from geography, is meaningless. History makes geography vital because it reveals the hills and plains, the rivers and seas as the homes of men and the theatre of stirring events. Geography gives history vividness and reality. In the light of Bible geography the men of the Bible stand out as real men who lived in our world, who thought out their truth, and wrought out their destiny as all nations must.

There are two forms of geographical study which apply to religious education, physical geography and historical geography. The first gives the setting and the second the sequence of events. Purely descriptive geography study is included in historical geography. Physical geography at once determines and interprets much of the history and many of the stories of the Bible. Confined within narrow limits by the desert, the sea, and the mountains, Palestine seems to be as distinct among the lands as its people among the

v

nations. The physical characteristics of the land are both
striking and of profound significance. It lay as a narrow
strip between the desert and the sea, a connecting link between the great civilizations of the Nile and the Euphrates.
The strip itself is broken into zones of widely different
character. Going inland from the sea, there is first a fertile
coast plain, which was a highway and a battleground for all
nations. Rising from the plain, along its entire length, as
the Catskills rise from the Hudson River Valley, and to the
same height, extends the central range. Beyond that is the
deep Jordan Valley. The fall from the Judean hills to the
Dead Sea is four-fifths of a mile in a distance of twenty
miles. Beyond the valley the eastern plateau stretches off
to the desert.

In all literalness the people of Israel were enisled among
the nations. In two directions they faced the desert and the
desert men. On the other sides the men and the life of all
the known world lured and imperilled them. The mèn of
Israel were at once in touch with all nations and yet, by
the paradox of history, were isolated from them by their
mountain homes and their natural bulwarks. The current
of the world's life flowed beside them, but they were suf-
ficiently separated to develop their own life.

The study of the physical geography will give the background and the setting for the history as nothing else will.
Historical geography will locate events both in place and
in time. To associate places with the events will invest the
places forever with reality. To associate the events with
places will show them in their relationship and sequence and
will thus be an invaluable aid to the memory. The most ef-
fective method of study is by means of such expressive ac-
tivities as Dr. Smith has outlined in the following pages. In
relief and in color work the four zones of Palestine, with their
determining influence on the history, will be made clear. By
coloring in political boundaries the pupil will learn the relation of the nations to each other, and the broad sweep of
history will be made clear. By placing events in order upon
a map, the details of history will be made clear.

MILTON S. LITTLEFIELD.

INTRODUCTION

For many years there has been a crying need for Bible Geography to make real and vivid the stirring stories of Sacred Writ. A number of large text-books, like the splendid volumes of George Adam Smith, John B. Calkin and Robert Laird Stewart, have been available; but their very size, thoroughness, and cost withal, have precluded their general study by the average lay teacher.

There has also been demand for a satisfactory course in this subject in the Subject-Graded Curriculum of progressive Sunday-schools. Only one such course has hitherto been produced, and that is too abstract and difficult, as well as lacking in picturesque interest.

We have endeavored in this little hand-book to provide for both of these requirements at a minimum cost. We have compiled a reading book, presenting the Holy Land in travel form, not separating the mountains, rivers, etc., into separate skeleton chapters; but fusing the entire physical picture, placing each in contiguous relations, and welding with the description, picture, and map of each city or site, the Biblical events in chronological order, associated with that locality, together with the Scripture reference. This has thus developed an excellent hand-book for the teachers and clergy.

In addition, for the school classes and individual pupils, we have appended to each chapter questions for clinching the reading and directions for manual and map work, tending to fix and test the results of study. They will be found invaluable for the adult reader as well.

For those who desire to pursue deeper research, or to acquire additional material for application as teachers and leaders of classes, a list of useful reference books is given.

WM. WALTER SMITH.

vii

REFERENCE BOOKS FOR FURTHER READING

For the advantage of teachers and pupils, who may have access to books from public or private libraries, or who may be able to purchase such, a list of the best books bearing upon Biblical Geography and Customs, as well as of the best Maps and Materials for Self-Expression, is appended below. Those marked with a star (*) are particularly commendable.

BOOKS ON BIBLICAL GEOGRAPHY.

*Historical Geography of the Holy Land. George Adam Smith. $6.00.
*Historical Geography of Bible Lands. John B. Calkin. $1.25.
*The Land of Israel. Prof. Robert Laird Stewart, D.D. $2.00.
The Rand McNally Bible Atlas. Rev. J. L. Hurlbut. $3.75.
*Historical Geography of Bible Lands. Richard Morse Hodge. $1.50.
*Biblical Geography and History. Charles Foster Kent, Ph.D. $1.90.
*The Geography of Bible Lands. Rena L. Crosby. $1.75.
*Bible Places. Rev. H. B. Tristram. $2.50.
*In the Master's Country. (Palestine) Miss Martha Tarbell. $1.
Sacred Geography and Antiquities. Rev. E. P. Barrows, D.D. $1.50.
*Peasant Life in Palestine. Rev. C. F. Wilson. $4.50.
Galilee in the Time of Christ. Rev. Selah Merrill. $1.50.
Today in Palestine. Rev. H. Dunning, Ph.D. $2.50.
*Out of Doors in the Holy Land. Rev. Henry J. Van Dyke, D.D. $2.50.

MAP BOOKS AND ATLASES WITHOUT DESCRIPTION.

*Littlefield Atlas. 32 maps in colors. 35c.

Pocket Atlas. 12 Maps. Good, but not up to date. Eiler. 10c.
Atlas of Bible Maps. George Adam Smith. $7.50.

WALL AND CLASS MAPS.

SMALL.

*Ways, Walks, and Words of the Master. Meigs. Gives place and event. Pa. 25c. Cloth, $1.50.
*New Testament Wall Map. Smith & Lamar. 50c.
*Collotype Relief Map. Armstrong. $5.75.
Class Map Charts, in case. Six maps. $3.75. Each map 75c.

LARGE.

*The Kent Wall Maps, eight sheets, 12 maps. Set $24.50. Each $3.50 and $3.
*The MacCalla Wall Maps. Old Test., New Test., Relief, Journeys of Christ, Jerusalem Picture. $2.75 each.
A. S. S. U. Cloth Maps, unmounted. Very accurate. Five maps. $2 each.

LARGE RELIEF.

*Relief Wall Map of Palestine. Burton. Paper maché.
*Palestine Exploration Fund Plaster Map. Palestine. Very fine.

OUTLINE WALL MAPS, PAINTED ON BLACKBOARD CLOTH.

Four Maps, Palestine, Sinai and Egypt, Mesopotamia, Roman World. $5 each.

OUTLINE CLASS MAPS ON PAPER.

THE LITTLEFIELD AND COMMISSION OUTLINE BIBLE MAPS.

All 2c. each, 12c. per dozen, $1 per 100, in any mixture.
a. Palestine in the world on Mercator Projection.
  1. Period of the Patriarchs and Exodus.
  2. Period of the Judges, 1270-1030.
  3. Period of the Kingdom of Saul, 1030-1010.
  4. Period of David and Solomon, 1000-937.
  5. Divided Kingdom to Revolution of Jehu, 937-842.
  6. Early Assyrian Period, 842-824.
  7. Syrian Conquests in Reign of Hazael, 814-797.
  8. Assyrian Conquests of Syria, 797-783.
  9. Period of Jeroboam II., 780-740.
  10. Conquests of Tiglath-Pileser III., 733-727.
  11. Fall of Israel and Period of Hezekiah, 727-695.
  12. Scythian Invasion and Period of Josiah, 639-608.
  13. Babylonian Period, 605-586.
  14. Period of the Exile, 586-536.
  15. Persian Period, 536-332.
  I. Palestine in Time of Christ.
  III. Palestine for Early Apostolic History.

*THE BAILEY SERIES.

Provides Maps and Key Maps. (Map 1) *The Hebrew World.* (Key 1) Positions of *Eastern Empires* in times of Abraham, Moses, David, Hezekiah, Zedekiah, and Nehemiah. (Key 1 a) *Eastern Empires* at times of Alexander, Eleazar II., the Maccabees, Cæsar, Christ, and Present Age. (Map 2) *Contour Maps of Palestine.* (Key 2) *Physical Maps of Palestine,* with Cross Sections. (Key 2 a Special, 2c.) The same,

small size, for coloring. (Key 2 a) *Location of Old Testament Places.* (Key 2 b) *Location of New Testament Places.* (Map 3) *Sinai, with Egypt and Palestine.* (Key Map 3*) *Routes of the Exodus and Wilderness Wanderings.* (Map 4) *Plain of Esdraelon.* (Key Map 4*) *Important New and Old Testament Places.* *Note that Keys 3 and 4 are on one sheet. (Map 5) *Contour Map of Jerusalem and Environs.* (Key Map 5) *City Walls and Important Old and New Testament Sites.* (New Map 5) The same in Half-tone. (Map 6) *The Early Christian World.* (Key Map 6) *The Journeys of St. Paul.*
These maps are accurate even to the smallest details, on good paper to take ink, crayon, or water color. Of uniform and standard size. A complete historical series of fifteen maps. (Two sizes, 7½ x 9½ inches, 2c. each; $1 per hundred. Small size, 4½ x 6⅞ inches, 1c. each; 10c. per dozen; 75c. per hundred. dozen; 75c. per 100.)
Key Maps, 5c. each sheet, in any quantity retail.)

*THE BLAKESLEE OUTLINE MAPS.

They may be used by any school or class desiring the best and most practical outline maps for Sunday School use.
Map No. 1. Large Outline Map of Palestine.
Map No. 10. Large Outline Map of the Roman Empire.
Size of these maps, 8 x 12½ inches. Printed on heavy bristol board for class use. They are to be developed by the class as the lessons are studied from week to week. The maps have a good surface to take ink, water color, or colored crayons. Either map, 10 cents each; 75c. per dozen, not prepaid.
Map No. 1A.
Map No. 10A.
These maps are the same as those of same number, Nos. 1 and 10 above, except that they are printed on regular thin map paper. These can be mounted

on cardboard or folded and used in the note-book. 5c. each; 30c. per doz.

Map No. 2. Egypt and Palestine. For tracing Mary and Joseph's journey to Bethlehem, the Flight into Egypt, and the Return to Nazareth.

Map No. 3. Palestine. Showing rivers, seas and boundaries.

Map No. 3B. Palestine. Showing rivers, seas, plains and mountains.

Map No. 4. Palestine, Showing the Principal Roads in the Time of Christ.

Map No. 5. Galilee. Showing mountains and plains, etc.

Map No. 6. Central Palestine. Showing mountains and plains, etc.

Map No. 7. Jerusalem and Vicinity. For the events in and around Jerusalem.

Map No. 8. Syria and Adjacent Countries. In S. Paul's early life, conversion and first missionary journey.

Map No. 9. Eastern Part of the Roman Empire. In S. Paul's missionary journeys and voyage to Rome.

These nine maps are each 4 x 5¾ inches, and are printed on good paper, to take ink, crayon or water color.

(Maps 2, 3, 3B, 4, 5, 6, 7, 8, 9, any assortment, 10c. per dozen; 75c. per 100.)

Colored Map of the Roman Empire, (2c. each, 15c. per dozen).

OUTLINE WALL MAPS IN ONE COLOR.

THE COOK SERIES.

Journeys of the Patriarchs, Canaan After the Conquest, Empire of David and Solomon, The Kingdoms of Israel and Judah, *Ancient Jerusalem, Palestine in Time of Christ, Journeys of Jesus. S. Paul's First Missionary Journey, Missionary Travels of the Apostle Paul.* Size 15 x 21 and 21 x 24 inches. On heavy *paper,* with eyelets for hanging, 15c. each; the same series on good *cloth,* 50c. each.

Roman World. Outline. Cloth. No. 151. S. S. Com. 50c.

GENERAL MATERIALS FOR HAND WORK

Sand Tables. "The Commission Table," the best made, tilting, revolving, zinc lined, 3 feet by 4 feet. $25.

Rockaway Sand. $2.25 per barrel.

Hailmann's Lentils, No. 458. 50c. per box of ¼ inch. 6 Colors. 1,000.

Crayola Crayons, 12 colors with key. Made up Expressly for Littlefield Old Testament Maps. 15c. a box.

Japanese Water Colors, on sheets, assorted colors. 15c. a sheet.

Paper Pulp, Green, Gray or White. 40c. a pound, dry. Made just for map-work.

Map Boards, for Paper Pulp Maps. Best Cypress. Every School NEEDS them. 60c. each.

Heavy, 14-ply Cards for Mounting Pulp Maps. 2c. each.

Plasticine, colored clay, brown, yellow, green, gray, blue. 50c. per pound.

Lane's Liquid Inks. All colors. $1.25 per doz.

Note Books, Ruled or Unruled. 144 pages, stiff cover. 25c. each. *The Same,* 72 pages, 15c. each.

Dennison's "a24" Stickers, for Picture Mounting. 25c. per box of 1,000.

Borders and Initial Letters for Coloring and Mounting Books. 2c. a sheet.

Binder's Boards for Note Taking. 9c. each. Made of Swedish Collerboard.

Religious Pictures. Tissot, Brown, Wilde, Union Press,

Perry, Eliott, Heidelberg, Sunday School Times Co. Card, etc., from ½c. to 8c. each.

Picture Catalog, listing 14,000 Bible Pictures, in Order, from over 35 Publishers, 9c. postpaid.

PICTURES OF PLACES AND SCENERY

A number of attractive pictures have been inserted in this Course. Separate pictures illustrative of the Places in these Chapters may be found in the list below. A Special Hand-book, with over 14,000 listings of Religious Pictures, arranged in Bible order, has been compiled by the Secretary of the New York Commission, as a manual of 122 pages, selling at 5 cents, postage, 4 cents extra. Every teacher ought to possess this Hand-book, and supply material for those who are able and willing to do advanced work in Illustrated Essays and Notebooks, inserting pictures, maps, drawings, etc., as is becoming now the custom in progressive Bible Class Work.

Picture Hand-book. Rev. Wm. Walter Smith, M. D., 5 cents, postage, 4 cents.

Bible Places. H. B. Tristram. (London, imp. by Gorham, cloth, $2.50 net.)

There are also fine series of Palestinian Views for the Stereoscope, by Underwood & Underwood, and White, at 20 cents each, with stereoscopes extra at 90 cents and $1.00.

All of these pictures are furnished in any assortment at the publishers' prices by the New York Sunday School Commission, Inc., 416 Lafayette Street, New York, the largest purveyors of religious pictures in the world.

See Note as to Lantern and Reflectoscope Lectures, page xxi.

Key Initials.

Bm., B.—Geo. P. Brown, Beverley, Mass.
Pm., P.—Perry Co., Malden, Mass.
    W.—Wilde Pictures, W. A. Wilde Co., Boston and Chicago.
    Co.—Cosmos Picture Co., New York.
   Cdr.—Card Series, Sunday School Commission.
    H.—Heidelberg Co., Philadelphia, Pa.
U. P.—Union Press, Philadelphia, Pa.
    T.—Tissot Co., S. S. Commission.
S. S. T.—The Sunday School Times Co., Philadelphia, Pa.
Scu. Smu.—Soule Co., Boston, Mass.
U. & U.—Keystone Co., Meadville, Pa.
A. A. C.—Detroit Photochrome Co., New York, N. Y.

The prices range thus:

Half-cent Pictures, Brown, Perry.
One and one-half and Two-cent Pictures, Perry, Brown, Wilde, Union Press, Heidelberg, Tissot, The Sunday School Times, Cosmos, Card.
Five-cent-Eight-cent Pictures, Perry, Brown, Cosmos.
Twenty-five-cent Pictures, Soule Co., Scu., Keystone.
Thirty-five-cent Pictures, Detroit Co., Soule Co.

LIST OF PICTURES.

PALESTINE.

Palestine, Relief Map of. U. & U. Ster. Ch. 7.

ANTIOCH.

Antioch, General View. S. S. T. 100.

ARABAH.

Arabah, The Region of. S. S. T. 202.

ATHENS.

Athens, Interior View Theatre of Bacchus. W. 458.
Athens, the Acropolis. A. A. C. 17292.
Athens, Mars' Hill. W. 457; U. & U. Ster. Greece (no number).

BABYLON.

Babylon, Restoration of. S. S. T. 102.
A Mound at the site of Ancient Babylon. S. S. T. 101.

BETHANY.

Bethany, Lower Road to. U. & U. Ster. Pal. 33.
Bethany, S. S. T. 238; W. 222; Co. 3104; A. A. C. 15045; B. 893; W. 223.
Bethany, Where Our Lord was Anointed by Mary, S. from eastern slope of Olivet. Palestine U. & U. Ster. Ch. 27, Pal. 36.
Bethany, Palestine, House of Mary and Martha. S. S. T. 250; U. & U. Ster. Pal. 37.
Bethany, Palestine, Tomb of Lazarus. W. 224; A. A. C. 15045; S. S. T. 249.
Bethany, Home in. S. S. T. 103.

BETHEL.

Bethel (General View). U. & U. Ster. Pal. 3334; Scu. 12351; A. A. C. 15054; S. S. T. 104.
Bethel, Palestine, The Gathering of Tares from Wheat, in the Stony Fields. U. & U. Ster. O. T. 3, Pal. 53.
Bethel, Stony ground of. S. S. T. 105.
Bethel and Dan. S S. T. 112.

BETHLEHEM.

Bethlehem (General View). W. 175; Co. 3109; Scu. 12352; Smu. 12352; A. A. C. Pan. s. 4515; A. A. C. ex. 3071; S S. T. 106.
Bethlehem, the Birthplace of Christ. Co. 3110; U. & U. Ster. Pal. 39; Scu. 12353; Smu. 12353.
Bethlehem, Birthplace of St. Helena. Scu. 12354; Smu. 12354.
Bethlehem, Peasants of the Neighborhood of. A. A. C. 15138.
Bethlehem, View within the Walls. A. A. C. 15143.
Young Women of Bethlehem in Costume. A. A. C. 15109.
Bethlehem, Group of Women of. A. A. C. 15114.
Bethlehem, Field of the Shepherd's Watch. W. 177; U. & U. Ster. O. T. 30; S. S. T. 107.
Bethlehem, Pools of Solomon. A. A. C. 15042.
Bethlehem, General View of the Well of David. A. A. C. 15038.
Bethlehem of Judea, where King David and Our Lord were Born. Palestine U. & U. Ster. Ch. 3.
Road to Bethlehem, from Jaffa Gate. Scu. 12347; Smu. 12347.
Bethlehem, David's Well, W. 176; A. A. C. 15038.

Bethlehem of Judea, A Barley
Harvest near. U. & U. Ster.
O. T. 29; Pal. 40.
Bethlehem, Church of the Nativ-
ity (Interior). U. & U.
Ster. Pal. 38.
Bethlehem, Grotto of the Nativ-
ity. W. 174; Scu. 12356;
Smu. 12356; A. A. C. 15041.
Bethlehem, Cave and the Cradle.
A. A. C. 15040.
Bethlehem, Manger at. U. & U.
Ster. Pal. 3314.
Bethlehem, Main Street of, lead-
ing from the Church of the
Nativity (looking N. W.).
Palestine U. & U. Ster. Ch. 2.
Bethlehem, Entry of Pilgrims on
Christmas Day. Co. 3108;
Scu. 12355; Smu. 12355; S.
S. T. 108.

BETH-SHAN.

Beth-Shan, where Saul's Body
was Taken. U. & U. Ster.
Pal. 3346.
Beth-Shan, up the Valley of Jez-
reel. U. & U. Ster. O. T. 32.
From Beth-Shan to Hill of
Moreh. U. & U. Ster. Pal.
3347.

CANA.

Cana of Galilee. W. 212; U. &
U. Ster. Pal. 80; Scu. 12357;
Smu. 12357; A. A. C. 15067;
S. S. T. 138.
Cana of Galilee, Palestine, In the
Court of a Village Home. U.
& U. Ster. O. T. 28; Ch. 17.
Canaan, The Borders of. S. S. T.
206.

CAPERNAUM.

Site of Capernaum and Sea of
Galilee. W. 213; S. S. T.
110.
Capernaum, The Ruins of. A. A.
C. 15073.
Galilee, Christ's Home in. U. &
U. Ster. Pal. 87.
A City Set on a Hill. S. S. T.
207.

CAESAREA PHILIPPI.

Old Gate to Caesarea Philippi, at
the foot of Mt. Hermon. Pal-
estine U. & U. Ster. Ch. 25;
Pal. 90.
Summer House at Caesarea Phil-
ippi; probably the "Taber-
nacles" referred to by St.
Peter. U. & U. Ster. Ch. 19;
Pal. 91.
Caesarea Philippi. S. S. T. 109.

CORINTH.

Corinth, General View. A. A. C.
18121; S. S. T. 111.
Site of Old Corinth, and Temple.
U. & U. Ster. Greece, 2413.
Corinth, The Temple in. U. &
U. Ster. Pal. 2444.

DAMASCUS.

Ancient Road from Palestine to
Damascus. U. & U. Ster.
Pal. 89.
Damascus, from Saliah. A. A. C.
15080.
Damascus, General View and Min-
aret of the Bride. A. A. C.
15081.
Abana River. "The Sweetened
Waters of Damascus." Syria
U. & U. Ster. O. T. 42; S.
S. T. 232.
Damascus, Stream of Barada.
A. A. C. 15086.
Damascus and Its Gardens. U. &
U. Ster. O. T. 43; Pal. 97.
Damascus, An Interior of a
House. U. & U. Ster. Pal.
99; A. A. C. 15087.
Damascus, The Court of a House.
A. A. C. 15088.
Church of St. John, Tomb of St.
John the Baptist. U. & U.
Ster. Pal. 3339.
Damascus, Tomb of St. John the
Baptist. Co. 3128; Scu.
12338; Smu. 12338.
Damascus, The Gate of the
"Street Called Straight." A.
A. C. 15083.
Damascus, "The Street Called
Straight." A. A. C. 15082;
U. &. U. Ster. Pal. 98.
Damascus, Wall Over which Paul
Escaped. A. A. C. 15084.
Damascus, An Oriental Prison.
S. S. T. 208.

DEAD SEA REGION.

Dead Sea, North Shore of. U. &
U. Ster. Pal. 45.
Dead Sea, On the North Shore of,
looking S. W. Palestine U.
& U. Ster. O. T. 6.
Dead Sea, Pisgah's Slopes over.
U. & U. Ster. O. T. 17.

DOTHAN.

Dothan, Plain of, where Joseph
was Sold to the Ishmaelites.
U. & U. Ster. O. T. 10;
Pal. 64.
Dothan, "Joseph's Well." U. &
U. Ster. Pal. 65.
Dothan, Joseph's Pit. S. S. T.
113.

EGYPT.

Egypt, Palm-Fringed Nile. U. &
   U. Ster. O. T. 14.
Egypt, Road to Pyramids. U. &
   U. Ster. O. T. 11.
Egypt, Pyramids and Sphinx.
   W. 179.
Egypt, Pyramids and Inundated
   Palms. W. 178.
Egypt, Ruins of the Granite Tem-
   ple, the Sphinx and Great
   Pyramid. U. & U. Ster. O.
   T. 12.
On Banks of River Nile. S. S. T.
   237.
The Suez Canal and the Red Sea.
   S. S. T. 231.
Egypt, Brick Store Chambers of
   Pithom, the City Built by
   Hebrew Bondsmen. U. & U.
   Ster. O. T. 15.
Egypt, Heliopolis. W. 181.
Egypt, Coptic Pilgrims from. U.
   & U. Ster. Pal. 3327.
Egypt, Cairo, Interior of Coptic
   Church. W. 316.
A Section of the Fertile Land of
   Goshen. S. S. T. 212.

EMMAUS.

Emmaus, Village of Amwas. U.
   & U. Ster. Pal. 7.

ESDRAELON.

Esdraelon, Plain of. Scu. 12360;
   Smu. 12360; S. S. T. 229.
Esdraelon, Laborers, Plain of.
   Scu. 12360; Smu. 12360; A.
   A. C. 15141.
The River Euphrates. S. S. T.
   233.

GALILEE.

Galilee, Sea of. W. 214; Smu.
   12370; S. S. T. 255.
Galilee, Sea of (View of Tiber-
   ias). W. 215.
Galilee, Sea of, Fishing. U. & U.
   Ster. Pal. 85.
Galilee, Fishing Boat on Sea of
   Tiberias. W. 308; S. S. T.
   210.
Galilee, Life on the Shores of, at
   Tiberias. U. & U. Ster. Ch.
   13; Pal. 84.
Galilee, Looking S. E. along the
   Eastern Shore of, where the
   Draught of Fishes were taken.
   U. & U. Ster. Ch. 36.
Sycamore Trees in Holy Land. S.
   S. T. 342.
Looking N. E. from the Mt. of
   Beatitudes to Capernaum and
   the Sea of Galilee. U. & U.
   Ster. Ch. 20; Pal. 81.
Palestine, Cornfield. S. S. T. 213.
Road Building in the Holy Land.
   S. S. T. 334.
Shepherd and His Dog. W. 243.
Druse Shepherd with a Lamb.
   W. 244.
On Mountains of Galilee. S. S.
   T. 209.

HARAN.

Haran, A Modern View of. S.
   S. T. 116.

GAZA.

Gaza. S. S. T. 115.

HEBRON

Hebron, General View. A. A. C.
   15043; A. A. C. Pan. s. 4537;
   S. S. T. 117.
Hebron, the Home of Abraham,
   Isaac and Jacob. U. & U.
   Ster. O. T. 4; Pal. 41.
Hebron, Abraham's Tree. Scu.
   12378; Smu. 12378; A. A. C.
   15044; S. S. T. 200.
Hebron, Tombs of the Patriarchs.
   A. A. C. 15144.
Hebron, Entrance to the Burial
   Place of Abraham. U. & U.
   Ster. Pal. 3317.
Mosque Machpelah, the Burial
   Place of Abraham. U. & U.
   Ster. O. T. 7; Pal. 42.
Hebron, King's Pool. U. & U.
   Ster. Pal. 3316.

ITALY (See also Rome).

Italy, Modern (Turner), B 1747.
   Florence, Rn. 5036; RL.
   55112.
Rome, Baptismal Font (St.
   Peter's). Rn. 746.
Pozzoull. W. 304.

JABBOK.

Jabbok Brook, where Jacob and
   Esau Met. U. & U. Ster.
   O. T. 9.

JAFFA (Joppa).

Jaffa, from the Sea. A. A. C.
   15001.
Jaffa, from the Garden. Scu.
   12363; Smu. 12363; A. A. C.
   15002.
Jaffa, the Joppa of Bible Times.
   U. & U. Ster. Pal. 1; Ch. 1.
Jaffa, House of Simon the Tan-
   ner. W. 302; U. & U. Ster.
   Pal. 3.
Jaffa, Boat and Boatmen of. Scu.
   12364; Smu. 12364; A. A. C.
   15134.
Jaffa, Bazar of. U. & U. Ster.
   Pal. 2.
Jaffa, Kirjath-jearin, Jerusalem
   Road. U. & U. Ster. Pal.
   1855.

JERESH.

Jerash in Gilead, on the Pathway of Jacob's Return to Canaan; most extensive ruins east of Jordan, looking north. U. & U. Ster. O. T. 8.

JERICHO.

Jericho, from the Plains. W. 210.
Jericho and Mt. Quarantana. W. 209.
Jericho, the Dead Sea. A. A. C. 15148-15050.
Jericho. W. 211, S. S. T. 119.
Jericho, General View. A. A. C. 15049.
Mountains of Judea from Jericho. U. & U. Ster. Pal. 48.
Wilderness of Judea. S. S. T. 244.
Jericho, on the road to—the Parable of the Good Samaritan. U. & U. Ster. Ch. 26.
Scene of the Good Samaritan Episode. Scu. 12369; Smu. 12369.
Khan-el-Ahmar, on the Road to Jericho. A. A. C. 15047.
Bedouin Robbers, Road to Jericho. U. & U. Ster. Pal. 3318.
Jericho, Modern. S. S. T. 118.

JERUSALEM.

From Mt. Ebal to Jerusalem. U. & U. Ster. O. T. 22.
Jerusalem, from Mt. Scopus. A. A. C. 15031.
Jerusalem, the City of the Great King, from Mt. Olives. U. & U. Ster. Ch. 30.
Jerusalem, the Holy City, from N. E., near the place from which it was first seen by Jesus. U. & U. Ster. Ch. 8.
Jerusalem, and the Mount of Olives. U. & U. Ster. Pal. 12; Ch. 32.
Jerusalem, Mount of Olives. Co. 3100.
Jerusalem, from Mt. of Olives. B. 997; W. 192-193; P. 1924; Co. 3101; U. & U. Ster. Pal. 18; A. A. C. 15030; A. A. C. Pan. med. 4516.
Jerusalem, A Glimpse of. S. S. T. 137.
Jerusalem, the Holy City, from the N. E. (showing the whole city). U. & U. Ster. O. T. 33.
Jerusalem, Valley of Jehoshaphat. W. 189; U. & U. Ster. Pal. 3280; A. A. C. 15035; S. S. T. 243.

Jerusalem, Valley of Hinnom. U. & U. Ster. 3281; S. S. T. 242.
Jerusalem, Brook Kedron. Scu. 12332; Smu. 12332.
Valley of Kedron and Village of Siloam from the South. U. & U. Ster. Pal. 14; O. T. 48.
Siloam. W. 220; Scu. 12374; Smu. 12374.
Siloam and the Tyrophean Valley. A. A. C. 15036.
Jerusalem. B. 997; U. & U. Ster. Pal 11; O. T. 46; A. A. C. ex. 3072.
Jerusalem, Wailing Place. W. 197; U. & U. Ster. O. T. 51; A. A. C. 15024.
Jerusalem, Walls and Golden Gate. W. 187; U. & U. Ster. Pal. 3287.
Jerusalem, Golden Gate. W. 204; A. A. C. 15025; S. S. T. 123.
Jerusalem, the Jaffa Gate. U. & U. Ster. Pal. 10; A. A. C. 15008.
Jerusalem, Inside the Jaffa Gate. W. 198; Scu. 12335; Smu. 12335.
Jerusalem, S. Stephen's Gate. W. 201; U. & U. Ster. Pal. 3289; A. A. C. 15026.
Jerusalem, Damascus Gate. W. 203; U. & U. Ster. Pal. 29; A. A. C. 15027.
Jerusalem, the Towers of David and Hippicus. W. 205; A. A. C. 15009.
Jerusalem, Street of the Tower of David. A. A. C. 15010.
Tower of David. U. & U. Ster. Pal. 9.
Jerusalem, Tower and Gate. S. S. T. 120.
Jerusalem, David's Castle. U. & U. Ster. Pal. 3288.
Jerusalem, Tomb of David. W. 184.
Jerusalem, Upper Room over Tomb of David. W. 191.
Jerusalem, Tomb of the Kings. W. 200; U. & U. Ster. Pal. 16; A. A. C. 15029.
Jerusalem, Tomb of Rachel. Scu. 12376; Smu. 12376; A. A. C. 15037.
"New Calvary" and "Tomb of Jeremiah." U. & U. Ster. O. T. 47.
Jerusalem, Jeremiah's Grotto. A. A. C. 15028; S. S. T. 220.
Jerusalem, Site of Solomon's Temple. W. 202; U. & U. Ster. Pal. 30; O. T. 35; A. A. C. 15018.

Solomon's Temple. W. 384; Scu. 12336; Smu. 12336.

Jerusalem, Stables of Solomon. Scu. 12348; Smu. 12348; U. & U. Ster. Pal. 3285.

Jerusalem, Tower of Antonia. W. 185; A. A. C. 15016.

Jerusalem, Site of the Tower of Antonia. A. A. C. 15021.

Jerusalem, Lane Leading to Herod's Palace. W. 196.

Street Leading to Herod's Palace. S. S. T. 214.

Herod's Temple. W. 385; Scu. 12338; Smu. 12338; S. S. T. 246.

Mt. Moriah, where the Temple Altar Stood. U. & U. Ster. Pal. 31.

Nero's Temple. Scu. 12339; Smu. 12339.

Jerusalem, Temple Area. S. S. T. 122.

Jerusalem, Mosque of Omar. W. 193; Co. 3141; U. & U. Ster. O. T. 36; Scu. 12341; Smu. 12341; A. A. C. 15019; A. A. C. ex. 3069.

Jerusalem, Mosque of Omar, Tribune of David. Scu. 12343; Smu. 12343.

Jerusalem, Rock of the Mosque of Omar. Scu. 12342; A. A. C. 15020.

Jerusalem, Mosque of El-Aksa. U. & U. Ster. Pal. 32; Scu. 12340; A. A. C. 15023.

Jerusalem, Pool of Bethesda. W. 188; B. 891; S. S. T. 248.

Jerusalem, Pool of Hezekiah. W. 288; U. & U. Ster. O. T. 44; A. A. C. 15011.

Pool of Siloam. W. 221; P. 1934; U. & U. Ster. Pal. 15; U. & U. Ster. Ch. 28; Scu. 12344.

Jerusalem, The Rich Man's House. W. 186.

Mount of Olives and Gethsemane. U. & U. Ster. O. T. 34; U. & U. Ster. Pal. 17; A. A. C. 15034.

Jerusalem, Garden of Gethsemane and Mt. of Olives, from the Eastern Wall. U. & U. Ster. Ch. 12.

Brook Kidron and Gethsemane. S. S. T. 252.

Garden of Gethsemane, Ancient Olive Trees. U. & U. Ster. Ch. 33; Pal. 35.

Garden of Gethsemane (View 1). W. 232; P. 1925; Co. 3103; A. A. C. 15033; A. A. C. ex. 3128.

Garden of Gethsemane (View 2). W. 231.

Garden of Gethsemane (View 3). W. 233.

Jerusalem, the Way to the Station. A. A. C. 15007.

Jerusalem, Arch of Ecce Homo. W. 190; A. A. C. 15017.

Jerusalem, Via Dolorosa (Way of Tears). U. & U. Ster. Pal. 3286; A. A. C. 15015.

House of S. Veronica, Jerusalem. W. 292.

Jerusalem, Via Dolorosa—Stations Ten and Eleven (Latin Altar). W. 296.

Jerusalem, Via Dolorosa—Stations Twelve and Thirteen (Greek Altar). W. 297; Scu. 12349; Smu. 12349; A. A. C. 15014.

Golgotha, or Calvary. W. 234.

Golgotha, Place of Skull. S. S. T. 253.

Jerusalem from Calvary. S. S. T. 257.

Jerusalem, Potter's Field. W. 199.

Fountain of the Virgin. W. 303; U. & U. Ster. Ch. 5; Pal. 72.

Tomb of the Virgin and Cave of Agony. A. A. C. 15032.

Interior of the Grotto of Agony. A. A. C. 15152.

Rock Tomb showing Stone Rolled Away. S. S. T. 241.

"Tomb of Our Lord," New Calvary, outside of Jerusalem. U. & U. Ster. Ch. 35; Pal. 27; S. S. T. 240.

Supposed Tomb of Our Lord. S. S. T. 240.

"The New Calvary," outside Damascus Gate. U. & U. Ster. Ch. 34; Pal. 26.

Jerusalem, Easter Procession of the Greek Patriarch, entering the Church of the Holy Sepulchre. U. & U. Ster. Pal. 22.

Jerusalem, Church of the Holy Sepulchre. W. 287; U. & U. Ster. Pal. 20; A. A. C. 15012.

Jerusalem, Church of the Holy Sepulchre (Gates). U. & U. Ster. Pal. 21; Scu. 12333; Smu. 12333.

Jerusalem, Stairway Leading to Church of Holy Sepulchre. W. 194.

Jerusalem, Interior of Church of Holy Sepulchre. W. 195; A. A. C. 15013.

Traditional Room of Our Lord's Supper. S. S. T. 251.

Jerusalem, Stone of Anointment, Church of Holy Sepulchre. U. & U. Ster. Pal. 3295.

Jerusalem, Beautiful Church of the Armenian Christians. U. & U. Ster. Pal. 24.

Mount of Olives, Church of the Ascension. W. 236.

Jerusalem, Pulpit of the Cadi-Borhan-ed-din. A. A. C. 15022.

Jerusalem, Road of the Captivity. Scu. 12346; Smu. 12346.

Jerusalem, Gate of the Prison of St. Peter. W. 300; Scu. 12345.

Rock of the Apostles. W. 298.

Jerusalem, Types of Jews in. A. A. C. 15129.

Jerusalem, Christian Street—Motley Life in the Holy City's Bazar District. U. & U. Ster. Pal. 19; O. T. 50.

"Unclean, Unclean"—Wretched Lepers Outside of Jerusalem. U. & U. Ster. Ch. 18; Pal. 34.

Jerusalem, Cattle Market Day in the Lower Pool of Gihon, Valley of Hinnom. U. & U. Ster. Pal. 13.

Sacrifices Near the Gates of Jerusalem. U. & U. Ster. O. T. 49; Ch. 31.

JEZREEL.

Jezreel, The Ruins. A. A. C. 15061.

Mt. Gilboa and Valley of Jezreel. U. & U. Ster. Pal. 3348.

An Old Watch Tower in Jezreel. U. & U. Ster. Pal. 3349.

Gideon's Battlefield and Hill of Moreh, North from Jezreel. U. & U. Ster. O. T. 26; Pal. 68.

"By the Side of Still Waters," on the Plain of Jezreel. U. & U. Ster. Ch. 6; Pal. 67.

JORDAN VALLEY.

Benias, Source of Jordan. W. 305; U. & U. Ster. O. T. 5; Pal. 88; Scu. 12350; Smu. 12350.

Tel-el-Kadi, Site of Dan and Source of the Jordan. A. A. C. 15074.

Plain of the Jordan. U. & U. Ster. O. T. 20; Pal. 50.

Plain of the Jordan, Southeast, from the Ruins of Ancient

Jericho. U. & U. Ster. Ch. 11.

Jordan River. P. 1921; Scu. 12367; Smu. 12367; A. A. C. 15051; S. S. T. 236.

Jordan, Palestine. P. 1922; S. S. T. 234.

Fords of the Jordan. W. 206; S. S. T. 235.

Jordan, Place of Baptism. A. A. C. 15052.

Baptizing in the Jordan. U. & U. Ster. Ch. 10; Pal. 47.

Bedouins of the Jordan District. A. A. C. 15125.

Ain Karin Convent—St. John's-in-the-Desert. W. 306.

Kadesh-Barnea. S. S. T. 221.

LEBANON.

Cedars of Lebanon. A. A. C. 15106.

LYDDA.

Lydda (The Biblical Lod), View from Southwest. U. & U. Ster. Pal. 5; A. A. C. 15003.

Lydda, Birthplace of England's Patron Saint, St. George. U. & U. Ster. Pal. 3278.

Lydda, Crusaders' Chapel Over Tomb of St. George. U. & U. Ster. Pal. 3279.

Lydda, Syrian Travelers near. U. & U. Ster Pal. 6.

MACHAERUS.

Machaerus. S. S. T. 124.

MAGDALA.

Magdala, Birthplace of Mary Magdalene. W. 214; A. A. C. 15072.

MAR-SABA.

Mar-Saba Convent. U. & U. Ster. Pal. 43; A. A. C. 15053.

MIZPAH.

Nebi-Samuel, or the Plain of Mispah. A. A. C. 15006.

From Mispah to Rama. U. & U. Ster. O. T. 21.

MOUNT OF BEATITUDES.

Mount of Beatitudes. W. 217; Scu. 12366; Smu. 12366; A. A. C. 15069; S. S. T. 225.

Mt. of Beatitudes and Mt. Tabor. U. & U. Ster. Pal. 3356.

West Shore of Galilee, Plain of Gennesaret, and Mt. of Beatitudes, from Bethsaida. U. & U. Ster. Ch. 23.

Bethsaida, Sea of Galilee, and Mt. of Beatitudes. U. & U. Ster. Pal. 86.

MOUNT CARMEL.

Mount Carmel. A. A. C. 15076;
  S. S. T. 222.
River Kishon and Mt. Carmel.
  U. & U. Ster. Pal. 76.
Carmel, the Mount of a Thousand
  Valleys. U. & U. Ster. Pal.
  1932.
Plain of Esdraelon and Mt. Car-
  mel. U. & U. Ster. Pal. 75.
Rock of Elijah's Altar, on Mt.
  Carmel. U. & U. Ster. O. T.
  40; Pal. 77.
Village of Dalieh, Mt. Carmel.
  U. & U. Ster. Pal. 1936.

MOUNT GERIZIM.

Mount Gerizim. Scu. 12373; Smu.
  12373; U. & U. Ster. Pal.
  58; A. A. C. 15057.
Mt. Gerizim, where the Samaritans Worshiped, and Steps
  to Jacob's Well, looking
  southwest. U. & U. Ster.
  Pal. 56.
From Mt. Ebal to Mt. Gerizim.
  U. & U. Ster. Ch. 15.
Sychar and Mt. Gerizim. U. &
  U. Ster. Pal. 3338.
Passover as Celebrated To-day by
  the Samaritans, Mt. Gerizim. U. & U. Ster. O. T. 16.

MOUNT GILBOA.

Gideon's Spring, Mt. Gilboa. U.
  & U. Ster. O. T. 25; Pal. 66.

MOUNT HERMON.

Mount Hermon and Plain of Tabor. A. A. C. 15149.
Mount Hermon, Where Jesus was
  Transfigured. Co. 3135; Scu.
  12365; Smu. 12365; A. A. C.
  15075.

MOUNT HOR.

Mount Hor. S. S. T. 223.

MOUNT NEBO.

From Mt. Nebo to the Promised
  Land. U. & U. Ster. O. T.
  18; Pal. 46; S. S. T. 224.

MOUNT TABOR.

Mount Tabor. A. A. C. 15063.
From Mt. Tabor to the Hill of
  Moreh. U. & U. Ster. Pal.
  70.
Looking South from Mt. Tabor
  to the Hill of Moreh. Palestine U. & U. Ster. O. T. 24.

NAIN.

Nain. W. 218; A. A. C. 15062.

Village of Nain and Mt. Tabor,
  looking northeast. U. & U.
  Ster. Ch. 21; Pal. 69; S. S.
  T. 125.

NAZARETH.

Nazareth. W. 183; B. 890; P.
  1923; U. & U. Ster. Pal. 71;
  A. A. C. 15064; A. A. C. ex.
  3073; S. S. T. 126.
Nazareth, across the Plain of
  Esdraelon. U. & U. Ster.
  Ch. 4.
From Mt. Ebal to Mt. Gerizim.
  U. & U. Ster. Ch. 15.
Nazareth, from Road to Cana. A.
  A. C. 15065.
Nazareth and Hill Country. W.
  182; Co. 3123.
Christian Girl of Nazareth. U. &
  U. Ster. Pal. 74.
Nazareth, the Place the People
  Wished to Throw Christ
  Over the Precipice. W. 183.
Nazareth, Interior of the Church
  of the Annunciation. A. A.
  C. 15151.
Carpenter Shop. S. S. T. 127.

PETRA.

Petra, An Altar of Baal. S. S.
  T. 201.

RAMAH.

Ramah, A Street in. U. & U.
  Ster. Pal. 52.
Ramah, A Woman of. U. & U.
  Ster. Pal. 3329.
Ramah, A Greek Priest Blessing
  the Village Children. U. &
  U. Ster. Ch. 29.

RAMLEH.

Ramleh Tower of the Forty Mar-
  tyrs. A. A C. 15005.
Ramleh, Panoramic View Taken
  from the Tower of the Forty
  Martyrs. A. A. C. 15004.
ROME (See also Italy).
Rome, Bird's Eye View from St.
  Peter's. A A. C. Pan. med.
  4555; U. & U. Ster. Rome 4.
Rome, Appian Way. P. 1743;
  Tba. 3050, 3051; W. 315;
  Tsa. 3050, 3051; Tpa 3050,
  3051; Rn. 614, 514a, 615;
  RL. 2024, 2025; A. A. C.
  3136; U. & U. Ster Rome 44.
Rome, the Coliseum. U. & U.
  Ster. Rome 30; A. A. C.
  1176; A. A C. 3138.
Rome, Sculpture, Showing the
  Seven-Branch Candlestick in
  the Arch of Titus. S. S. T.
  337.

Rome, Palatine. A. A. C. 3135.
Rome, General View from the Palatine. A. A. C. 8577.
Rome, the Forum from the Palatine. A A. C. 8587.
Rome, the Forum, U. & U. Ster. Rome 1991; A. A. C. 1177.
Rome, the Parthenon. A. A. C. 8573; U. & U. Ster. Rome 23.
Rome, St. Paul's House. S. S. T. 256; P. 1769.

SAMARIA.

Samaria, General View. W. 229; Scu. 12368; Smu. 12368; U. & U. Ster. O. T. 39; A. A. C. 15058; S. S. T. 130.
Samaria, Herod's Capital City. U. & U. Ster. Pal. 3340
Samaria, Ancient City of. U. & U. Ster. 62; S. S. T. 131.
House-tops of Samaritan Houses. W. 227.
Samaria, the Colonnade. A. A. C. 15059.
Samaria, Threshing Floor, at. U. & U. Ster. Pal. 3341.
Road from Samaria to Jerusalem. S. S. T. 239.
The Inn of the Good Samaritan. S. S. T. 219.
Samaria, Group of Lepers. W. 228.
Samaria, Jacob's Well. W. 312; S. S. T. 247.
A Samaritan Woman at Jacob's Well. U. & U Ster. Ch. 16; Pal. 57.
Mt. Ebal and Joseph's Tomb. U. & U. Ster. Pal. 3375
Road from Samaria to Jenin. U. & U. Ster. Pal. 3345.
Herod's Street of Columns. U. & U. Ster. Pal. 63.

SHECHEM.

View from Mt. Ebal, S. W., over Shechem, Mt. Gerizim and the Seacoast Plain to Joppa. U. & U. Ster. O. T. 2.
Nablous (Shechem). W. 226; A. A. C. 15055; S S. T. 133.
Nablous and Mt. Gerizim. Scu. 12373; Smu. 12373; U. & U. Ster. Pal 58; A. A. C. 15057.
Shechem, Mount Ebal. Scu. 12372; Smu. 12372; U. & U. Ster. O. T. 38.

Shechem, from Mt. Ebal. U. & U. Ster. O. T. 23.
Nablous, Vale of Nabulus. A. A. C. 15056.
Shechem, Grave of Joseph. U. & U. Ster. Pal. 3336.
Samaritan High Priest and Pentateuch Roll, Supposed Writing of Aaron's Great-grandson, Shechem. Palestine U. & U. Ster. O. T. 45; Pal. 59; S. S. T. 336; S. S. T. 335.

SHILOH

Shiloh, Resting Place of the Ark. U. & U. Ster. Pal. 54.
Shiloh. S. S. T. 134.

SIDON.

Sidon. Scu. 12375.
Traditional Hill of the Swine. S. S. T. 215.
Ancient Citadel in the Sea of Sidon. Syria U. & U. Ster. Pal. 93.

SYRIA (See also Damascus)

House in Syria Built upon a Rock. S. S. T. 217.
Baalbek, Syria. U. & U. Ster. Pal. 3396; U & U. Ster. Pal. 96.
Syria, Ruins of Baalbek. U. & U. Ster. Pal. 95.
Syria, Mount Lebanon. U. & U. Ster. Pal. 94.
Tomb of Hiram, King of Syria. U. & U. Ster. 3390.

THESSALONICA

Salonica, Ancient Thessalonica. U. & U. Ster. Greece 2467.

TIBERIAS.

Tiberias, View of Tiberias. W. 215; U. & U. Ster. Pal. 82.
Tiberias, Panoramic View. A. A. C. 15069.
Tiberias, View from the Fortress. A. A. C 15070.
Tiberias, Fisherman's Boat on the Lake. U. & U. Ster. Pal. 83; A. A. C. 15071; S S. T. 351.

TYRE

Tyre, Harbor. U. & U. Ster. Pal. 3388.
Tyre. A. A. C. 15078; S. S. T. 136.
Ruins of Ancient Tyre—Wonderful fulfillment of Prophecy. U. & U. Ster. Ch. 24; Pal. 92.

The N. Y. S. S. Commission has also prepared a special Typewritten Stereopticon Lecture with about 100 Slides, covering the material and places in this book. Separate Slides may be purchased at 50 cents each, plain; $1.50 each, colored. The ½ cent and 1½ cent Prints, noted above, also furnish a complete outfit for Opaque Projectors.

NOTE

There is a very beautiful Set of some 60 or more Postcards of Palestine in colors, recently imported by the Sunday School Commission from Jerusalem, selling at $2.75 per set of fifty, postage 10 cents extra. We recommend these both for general teaching and for Reflectoscope Work. Most of them are Colored Pictures of Sites and Views, although quite a few are beautiful illustrations of Native Customs and Costumes.

CONTENTS

FOREWORD v

INTRODUCTION vii

REFERENCE BOOKS FOR FURTHER READING ix

PICTURES OF PLACES AND SCENERY xiii

LIST OF MAPS IN APPENDIX xxv

CHAPTER I
THE BIBLE WORLD I

CHAPTER II
THE ZONES OF PALESTINE 6

CHAPTER III
THE THIRD ZONE OF PALESTINE. SAMARIA 12

CHAPTER IV
THE THIRD ZONE OF PALESTINE. CONTINUED. JUDEA . 18

CHAPTER V
JERUSALEM AND ITS ENVIRONS 22

CHAPTER VI
JERUSALEM, CONTINUED. FOURTH QUARTER AND SUR-
ROUNDING ROADS 28

CHAPTER VII
THE FOURTH ZONE OF PALESTINE. THE JORDAN VALLEY
TO THE GHOR 33

xxiii

CHAPTER VIII
THE REMAINDER OF THE JORDAN VALLEY 39

CHAPTER IX
THE FIFTH ZONE OF PALESTINE. THE EASTERN TABLE
LAND 44

CHAPTER X
THE SIXTH ZONE 51

CHAPTER XI
THE EASTERN EMPIRES 54

CHAPTER XII
THE LANDS OF ST. PAUL'S LABORS.—ASIA MINOR, THE
MEDITERRANEAN, GREECE, ROME 59

APPENDIX
KEY TO THE LOCATION OF EVENTS IN OUR LORD'S LIFE AS
NOTED ON JOURNEY MAPS 69

FORTY-ONE BIBLE MAPS 77-116

INDEX 117

LIST OF MAPS IN APPENDIX

1. The World on Mercator Projection. Outline.
2. Physical Map of Palestine. Relief.
3. Western Asia in Early Times. Outline.
4. Egypt, Sinai, and Canaan. Outline.
5. The Period of the Patriarchs. Colored.
6. Route of the Exodus. Colored.
7. Period of the Tribal Settlements. Approximate, according to Book of Joshua. Colored.
8. Period of the Judges, 1270-1030. Colored.
9. Period of the Kingdom of Saul, 1030-1010. Colored.
10. Period of David and Solomon, 1000-937. Colored.
11. Divided Kingdom to Revolution of Jehu, 937-842. Colored.
12. Syrian Conquests in Reign of Hazael, 814-797. Colored.
13. Assyrian Conquests of Syria, 797-783. Colored.
14. Period of Jeroboam II., 780-740. Colored.
15. Conquests of Tiglath-Pileser III., 733-727. Colored.
16. Fall of Israel and Period of Hezekiah, 727-695. Colored.
17. Scythian Invasion and Period of Josiah, 639-608. Colored.
18. Babylonian Period, 605-586. Colored.
19. Period of the Exile, 586-536. Colored.
20. Persian Period, 536-332. Colored.
21. The Thirty Years of Private Life of Our Lord. Colored.
22. The Opening Events of Christ's Life. Colored.
23. The Early Judean Ministry. Colored.
24. The Galilean Ministry, First Period. Colored.
25. The Galilean Ministry, Second Period. Colored.
26. The Galilean Ministry, Third Period. Colored.
27. The Perean Ministry. Colored.
28. The Appearances of the Forty Days. Colored.
29. S. Philip's Journey. Colored.
30. Saul's Journey. Colored.
31. S. Peter's Journey. Colored.
32. Journeys of S. Barnabas and S. Paul. Colored.
33. S. Paul's First Missionary Journey. Colored.
34. S. Paul's Second Missionary Journey. Colored.
35. S. Paul's Third Missionary Journey. Colored.
36. S. Paul's Voyage to Rome. Colored.
37. Road Map of Palestine. Outline.
38. Ancient Jerusalem. Outline.
39. Jerusalem in Nehemiah's Time. Outline.
40. Modern Jerusalem. Colored.
41. Modern Palestine, with Ancient and Modern Cities. Colored.

CHAPTER I

THE BIBLE WORLD

What the Bible World Includes. Speaking generally, one may say that all the principal events noted in the Bible occurred within lands bordering on the eastern portion of the Mediterranean Sea, and countries almost adjacent. The Old Testament history (Appendix) is embraced between the four great seas of Western Asia,—the *Mediterranean,* the *Black,* the *Caspian,* and the *Persian Gulf.* The history of the life of Christ lies in *Palestine proper.* The Book of Acts and the early apostolic history includes *Palestine, Syria, Asia Minor,* and the *Roman Empire,* bordering on the Mediterranean. The Old Testament world runs from the mouth of the Nile to the Persian Gulf on the south (see maps throughout) and from Mount Sinai to Mount Ararat, near the Caspian Sea. Its total extent is about 1,400 miles east and west, and about 900 miles north and south. Its land area is about 1,110,000 square miles, or one-third that of the United States proper. Of this area, however, more than two-thirds is a vast desert, so that the occupied land amounts in extent to less than one-eighth of the United States.

Chief Physical Features of the Old Testament World. Looking at the map (Appendix) we see, in *Egypt* the *River Nile,* with its broad Delta; then traveling eastward, the *Gulf of Suez,* the *Sinai Peninsula,* containing the *Desert of Paran;* and next the *Gulf of Akabah.* In Palestine, if we cross from Joppa, we pass in order through the *Maritime Plain,* a *Central Range of Mountains,* the *Jordan River* and its wide valley, the *Eastern Range of Mountains in Gilead,* then the *Arabian Desert,* the *Euphrates River, Mesopotamia* and *Chaldea,* the *Tigris River,* the huge *Zagros Range of Mountains,* and finally the land of *Media.* (All these places should be looked

1

up on the map and sketched in an outline map, made by the student.)

Limits and Names of Palestine. The region is rather indefinite, especially in differing times in history. The early name was *Canaan* (Num. 13 : 29), from the Canaanites, who lived there before the entrance of the Hebrews. When the ancient Hebrews took possession they called it the *Land of the Hebrews,* or the *Land of Israel.* Canaan referred to the country between the Jordan and the Mediterranean (the Great Sea) and between Mount Lebanon and the Southern Desert. Palestine is often given as a title to this section *Palestine* comes from à Greek word used to designate Philistia (Psa. 60 : 8), originally in Greek "Palaistine," and later altered by the Romans to Palestina. Philistia meant the land inhabited by the Philistines. This region of Palestine covers only 6,600 square miles, smaller than Massachusetts by some 1,200 square miles.

Palestine proper embraces both Canaan and the land east of the Jordan, often loosely termed *Gilead,* covering in all about 12,000 square miles, or equal to Massachusetts and Connecticut. Another name, given by the prophet Zechariah (Zech. 2 : 12), is *the Holy Land.* (See also Gen. 13 : 14-17 and Deut. 7 : 6.) In Hebrews 11 : 9, it is called the *Land of Promise.* (See Num. 34.) Western Palestine has about the same area as the state of New Jersey and about the shape of New Hampshire. It would extend from New York up the Hudson to within about ten miles of Albany. Palestine lay at almost the precise center of the then known world. If one were to draw a circle of 1,600 miles diameter, with Jerusalem as the focus, all the great cities of ancient times would be included,—Rome, Athens, Ephesus, Nineveh, Babylon, Memphis, Thebes, and Alexandria. It was a land shut in by mountains, which in turn shut out many enemies. Nevertheless it was the great highway between Egypt and Babylon, because, lying between both, the caravan routes passed through it with the commerce of these two mighty countries. One of the common Old Testament modes of limiting the extent of Canaan was by referring to it as "From Dan to Beersheba" (Judg. 20 : 1).

In Northern Africa (Egypt) and the Sinaitic Peninsula, we should note the following fixed features: EGYPT lies along the two sides of the river Nile. There have always been two Egypts, Northern and Southern. *Northern* or *Lower Egypt* lies in the *Nile Delta,* triangular in shape, a huge, splendid garden, with the richest soil of the then known world, the grain lands of the Roman Empire. *Southern* or *Upper Egypt* winds along the Nile Valley, from two to ten miles wide, with barren hills on either side, beyond which lay desert. These two Egypts were always so separate that the very crowns, worn by the kings, were double. The main stream of the Nile is known as the *White Nile,* while the *Blue Nile* flows into it in Nubia, rising far back in Abyssinia. *The Land of Goshen* lay southeast of the Delta. It was the home of the Israelites during their long sojourn in Egypt as slaves. The only cities of Bible note in Egypt were *Heliopolis,* called *On* in the Scriptures, on the eastern branch of the Delta (Gen. 41 : 45, 50; 46 : 20), *Alexandria,* in later times the metropolis of Africa (Acts 6 : 9, 18 : 24, 27 : 6, 28 : 11); while *Thebes* was the chief city of Upper Egypt, and its capital.

The great SINAITIC PENINSULA lies between Egypt and the Gulf of Suez on the one side and the arm of the Red Sea known as the Gulf of Akaba on the other. It forms a huge triangular desert. To the northern end lies a plain of white sand, *the wilderness of Shur,* then below a barren tableland of limestone, known as *the Wilderness of Paran,* "the great and terrible wilderness" of the Forty Years' Wanderings of the Israelites (Deut. 1 : 19). It is still called *Et Tih,* "the Wandering," and is crossed by two drear caravan routes, marked by dry bones of victims to its scourge. At its lowest point is the *Wilderness of Mount Sinai,* bordered by *the Wilderness of Sin,* not to be confounded with the *Wilderness of Zin,* lying just below the foot of the Dead Sea. Much discussion has arisen as to the site of *Mount Sinai,* the terms Horeb and Sinai being seemingly used interchangeably. Several peaks have been claimed, presuming that Horeb applied to the range of Mountains and Sinai to a particular peak. *Jebel Musa,* the Mountain of Moses, is the

Mountain of the Law, according to local tradition. *Ras es Sufsafeh* has the preference of many modern writers, and, if the mountain lay at all in the south, is the most likely from its nature. The most recent critical research, favoring the shorter route of the Exodus straight across the Peninsula to the head of the Gulf of Akaba, places the Mountain of the Law near that spot.

The places of Bible interest are *Rameses* in Goshen, the starting-point of the Exodus; *Succoth* directly south a short space; *Etham* on the edge of the Lake above the Gulf; *Pi-hahiroth* and *Baal-Zephon* near the Gulf. The sites of other places mentioned as *Marah, Elim,* and *Rephidim* are altogether uncertain. (Read Exodus 12-14; Numbers 33.)

Physical Palestine in Detail. It is most important that we study the physical geography of the Holy Land in quite some detail, for, while it is true in general that geography has always left its stamp upon the history and character of mankind, it is especially true of the Hebrews, for no people of antiquity ever lived in closer contact with Nature than did they. We shall find this study of entrancing interest, for Palestinian characteristics are reflected in almost every psalm, prophecy, and parable given us in Holy Writ. "The Cedars of Lebanon, Mount Hermon, the flowing springs, the restless sea, the roaring lion, the eagle, the lily, even the sparrows" are all pictured in Bible literature. As we traverse the land, the gloomy Valley of Michmash becomes the scene of the heart-stirring attack of Jonathan upon the Philistines, that gave the Hebrews their independence from the giants. On the Plain of Megiddo, Thothmes III, Necho, and Napoleon have trodden the same paths of battle. Here is a land that Nature destined to be the great highway over which would pass and repass nations upon nations, bent on war or commerce. As we witness the location of the Hebrew homes, high on towering mountains, we can see God's plan for seclusion and education, a preparation for their contribution to the world or the world's greatest religion. And it has been the physical contour and characteristics of this land of sacred memories that has moulded the life of the dwellers among the mountains and valleys and plains that mark its face. What at first seems but a confused, unthreaded series of valleys and hills is revealed on closer inspection as an orderly, naturally-developed set of *six zones*, each with a type of life and character peculiar to its environment, each contributing directly to the special production of a distinct race and religious standard. We shall study each zone and include in each its own mountains, rivers, valleys, and cities, thus connecting them together in orderly pictorial sequence.

Questions and Manual Work on Chapter I.

1. On a world outline map (Sunday School Commission Mercator Map, 2c. each) color in green crayon or water tint *Egypt,* in red *Palestine,* in indigo *Mesopotamia,* in yellow *the lands beyond the Tigris eastward,* in violet *Greece,* in black *Asia Minor,* in orange *Italy.* Put all *rivers* and *seas* in blue. Leave all the rest blank.

2. Write the names and origin of all names of Palestine.

3. Print on the map the chief physical features of the Old Testament world.

4. Copy an outline map of Palestine (S. S. Commission) or a map in this book, or trace it if you cannot copy it.

5. Why is the study of Bible geography of value? How did the land determine Bible history?

CHAPTER II

THE ZONES OF PALESTINE

Detailed Study of Zones I, II, and part of III.

The First Zone—THE MARITIME PLAIN. Here lie the sea-coast plains, along the eastern coast of the Mediterranean. At the northern portion this is a narrow strip of land, the cradle of those ancient mariners the Phoenicians; a fertile region, but too small for aught but a meager population. Its principal cities were *Tyre* and *Sidon*. (See S. Mark 7 : 24.) It was in this locality that Christ met the Syrophoenician woman.

In Syria, beyond the boundaries of Palestine proper, are two of the lofty parallel ranges of mountains, *the Lebanon* and the *Anti-Lebanon*. The former has an average height of 7,000 feet, and is the starting-point of all the great Palestinian systems of mountains. The latter is noted for *Mt. Hermon*, which rises 9,200 feet, and is generally regarded as the *Mount of the Transfiguration* of Christ. In its neighborhood is *Cæsarea Philippi*, which we believe to be the farthest limit north of our Lord's missionary work. Through these mountains flows *the Litany River*, in Bible times termed the *Leontes*.

Farther south, the *Plain of Acre* broadens out till it ends at *Mount Carmel*, or *the Carmel range of mountains, as it really* is. Then comes the *River Kishon*, at the foot of this mountain range, "that ancient river" (Judg. 5 : 21). Here Deborah ruled and Sisera, captain of Jabin's army, was delivered into her hands. (Judg. 4 : 4-15.) Here Elijah slew the prophets of Baal. (1 Kings 18 : 40.) Next is *Carmel*, reaching 1,750 feet high; but sloping down to 500 as it meets the sea. Here Elijah lived (1 Kings 18 : 18 : 20); here he met Ahab; and here he won the victory for Jehovah.

See opp. p. 6

See opp. p. 6
See opp. p. 6

TYRE

SIDON
From the Sea

MT. CARMEL

RIVER KISHON
Photo by S. U. Mitman

JOPPA, OR JAFFA

HOUSE OF SIMON
Photo by Rev. S. U. Mitman

CAESAREA IN PALESTINE
Copyrighted by Underwood & Underwood

CAESAREA
St. Paul's Prison

Below Carmel stretches the ever-widening fertile *Plain of Sharon,* with its forests and fruitful fields, its undulating flower-beds of vernal beauty, dotted with the "Tents of Kedar." Solomon refers to "the rose of Sharon" (Song of Sol. 2 : 1). Isaiah refers to it frequently for its beauty and rich fertility (Isa. 33 : 9; 35 : 2; 65 : 10). A little farther south, it widens to twenty-five miles, and was the home for centuries of the warlike Philistines (from which the name Palestine, as we have said, was derived). In Old Testament times it was never inhabited by Hebrews. Even in Christ's time, though many Jews inhabited it, they felt like strangers in it. It was in all ages a famous war-path. Over it marched the armies of Thothmes, Rameses, Sennacherib, Cambyses, Alexander the Great, Pompey, and Napoleon. Like all coast plains, it was exposed to attack from all sides. This will account for the bravery developed in the hardy Philistine warriors. *The sea-coast* is remarkably regular, there being only one promontory or cape, where Carmel juts into the sea. There are few good harbors. We have noted Tyre and Sidon. Below are *Ptolemais, Cæsarea,* and *Joppa* (Jaffa). The See opp. p. 7 sea is shallow all along the coast. *Cæsarea* was built by See opp. p. 7 Herod in Roman times, and was of unusual beauty and wealth. S. Paul was a prisoner here for two years on his last voyage See opp. p. 7 to Rome. From Joppa, Jonah set sail to escape God (Jonah 1 : 3) and centuries later S. Peter had his vision of the sheet, and his call to Cornelius and the Gentile world (Acts 10 : 1-16). At *Lydda* (now Lod or Lud), S. Peter preached the See opp. p. 10 gospel. (Acts 9 : 32.) In PHILISTIA, the chief cities are *Gaza,* in the southwest corner, three miles from the sea, See opp. p. 10 mentioned from earliest times down into the book of Acts and still a city to-day (see Gen. 10 : 19; Josh. 10 : 41; 11 : 22; 13 : 3; 15 : 47; Judg. 1 : 18; 16 : 21; Acts 8 : 26). The reference in Acts is to the noteworthy baptism of the Ethiopian eunuch. *Ashkelon* was noted in Philistine times and in the days of the Crusades. *Ashdod* was the chief seat of the worship of Dagon, the fish-god. *Ekron* was the last resting-place of the Ark previous to its return. *Gath,* now unknown as to site, was the home of Goliath the giant. (1 Sam. 17 : 4, 23; 1 Sam. 5 : 10.)

The Second Zone—THE SHEPHELAH. This is the district composed of low foothills lying between the Maritime Plain and the Central Uplands. It is an open, rolling region. Here in the days of the Judges raged the intermittent warfare between the lowlanders and the highlanders. These foothills are about 500 feet only above sea-level. In the early times these combatants were Israelites and Canaanites; later, they were Israelites and Philistines; then the Maccabees fought here with the Syrians; and in the time of the Crusades Richard of England and Saladin the Saracen led the opposing armies. The *Shephelah proper* lies only between Beersheba and the Valley of Aijalon. The word means Low Country, being lower than the neighboring mountains to the East. (See 2 Chron. 28 : 18.) *The Valley of Aijalon* runs across the top of the Shephelah, just north of Jerusalem. Along this valley, Joshua pursued the Amorites, at the time when he bade the sun to stand still. (Josh. 10 : 1-14.) Through this valley, the Philistines came to attack King Saul, when Jonathan repelled them. (1 Sam. 13, 14.) *Gezer,* an important city of which King Horam was ruler, is at this valley, on the surrounding hills. (Josh. 10 : 33; 12 : 12.) Next, south from the Shephelah, lies the *Valley of the Sorek,* where Samson, born at *Zorah,* worked his wonderful deeds. Here too was *Timnath,* where Samson's first love dwelt. South of Sorek, was *Beth-Shemesh,* to which the ark was brought from Ekron, and there still spread out wheat-fields like those the lowing kine passed through. (1 Sam. 6.) A little farther south lies the *Valley of Elah,* a level plain, the battlefield where David killed the giant Goliath (1 Sam. 17). Near by is the *Cave of Adullam,* where David hid with his four hundred followers. (1 Sam. 22.) At the southern boundary of the Shephelah is the *Brook Besor,* while farther south still is the city of *Beersheba,* which marks the extreme limits of the Land of Israel. It was at different times the home of Abraham, Isaac, and Jacob. It lay on the caravan highway, and was noted for its seven great wells.

The Third Zone—THE CENTRAL PLATEAU. This is the rough, jagged, towering mountainous system, running north and south, between the Shephelah and Maritime Plain and the Valley of the Jordan River. It has three distinct divisions, each with clearly marked characteristics. They are known on New Testament maps as Galilee, Samaria, and Judea.

GALILEE is the most northern division. It is enriched by the streams that flow from Mt. Hermon, making it well-watered and very fertile. *The Leontes,* rising near ancient Baalbac, flows south through Coele-Syria (Hollow Syria) 120 miles to the sea. Numerous brooks or wadies follow in parallel lines southward, ending with the River Kishon, at Carmel's base. The name Galilee means a round object or region, i.e., well-defined and distinct. It was thus first given to a small portion or spot and then extended to include more. (Josh. 20 : 7.) At first nations not of Israelitish descent dwelt in this region. Hence it was frequently called "Galilee of the Gentiles." (Isa. 9 : 1.) The district reaches north to the Leontes, east to the Lake of Galilee and south to the Plain of Esdraelon. Upper Galilee was much higher than Lower Galilee, its mountains rising to 3,000 feet, while almost all mountains in Lower Galilee are below 2,000 feet. The mountains are in most cases broad plateaus, broken by wide, deep valleys. Of the mountains of Galilee, *Mount Tabor* See opp. p. 10 (over 1,800 feet high), on the northeast of Esdraelon, shows out clearly. (Psa. 89 : 18; Jer. 46 : 18.) Here Deborah and Barak met Sisera (Judg. 4 : 6-14). (See also River Kishon, First Zone.) *Little Hermon* (1,800 feet) is known as the *Hill of Moreh.* (Judg. 7 : 1.) It is on the Plain, southwest of the Sea of Galilee. *Endor* is on the northern slope. The witch that Saul visited lived here. (1 Sam. 28 : 7-25.) Seven or eight miles away is *Gilboa,* where Saul camped. In Old Testament times the tribes of Asher and Naphtali settled in this section. After the early settlement there is little mention of Galilee for years, until Christ's time, when a large portion of His ministry was located here. Of the cities, the following are of most importance :

Kedesh (*Kedesh-Naphtali*) was both a city of refuge and a fortified city, west of the head of *Lake Huleh* (*Lake Merom*). It was the site of the old Temple of the Sun, the ruins of which are still there, and the capital or sanctuary of the great tribe of Naphtali. It was also the home of Barak. (See Josh. 20 : 7; 21 : 32; Judg. 4 : 10; 2 Kings 15 : 29; Judg. 4 : 6; Josh. 19 : 32.) *Shunem* lies about eight miles south of Mount Tabor. It belonged to the tribe of Issachar, and is noted for the story of Elisha given in 2 Kings 4 : 8. Three miles south of Kedesh is *Hazor,* once a royal town, now a collection of broken cisterns. It is of note in the Bible. (Josh. 11 : 10; 2 Kings 15 : 29.)

See opp. p. 10 In Lower Galilee lies *Nazareth,* the home of S. Mary the Virgin and S. Joseph her husband; the place where our Lord was reared to manhood. Although shut in by hills, it was the great junction town at which converged all the many caravan routes from lower Palestine and Egypt into Asia Minor and Assyria. From the heights of the Nazareth Range near by can be seen many of the famous places in upper Palestine. The scene of more than twenty battles, most momentous in the history of the Chosen People, lay before our Master's vision as he climbed His native hills around. Here he dwelt See opp. p. 11 until thirty years of age. *Cana of Galilee* was a little north See opp. p. 11 of Nazareth and nearer to *Capernaum,* which lay on the Lake of Galilee. It was the town of Christ's first miracle (the wedding feast) and also the home of Nathanael the disciple. See opp. p. 11 (See S. John 2 : 11; 4 : 46; 2 : 1; 21 : 2.) *Nain* is on the northwest of Little Hermon. Here Christ raised the widow's son to life. (S. Luke 7 : 11.)

The highest point in Galilee is *Mt. Jebel Jermuk,* northwest of the Sea of Galilee, 4,000 feet high. A few miles west of the middle of the same Lake stands the *Kurun Hattin* or *Horns of Hattin,* a mountain 1,200 feet high, with two peaks. It is known as the *Mount of the Beatitudes,* and on its side our Lord preached his famous sermon on the Mount. Authorities differ as to this site. (S. Matt. 5, 6, 7.) Hattin is also the historic landmark that overlooks the spot where the army of the Crusaders made its last memorable stand, and was almost utterly annihilated by the vengeful hosts of Saladin, in 1187 A. D. Esdraelon itself we shall consider as the Sixth Zone of Palestine.

LYDDA

GAZA ROAD
Photo by Williams, Brown & Earle

MT. TABOR
Plains of Esdraelon

NAZARETH

CANA OF GALILEE

SITE OF CAPERNAUM

NAIN
Photo by S. U. Mitman

BETHEL

Questions and Manual Work on Chapter II.

1. Learn to make a map of Palestine quickly. Fold a sheet of paper of the proportion of 8 x 12 inches in three divisions lengthwise. Unfold and again fold three times sideways. This gives nine squares. Draw the coast line of the Carmel Range in the upper middle square. Continue coast line to the middle of right-hand center square, lower edge. In lower right-hand corner of upper middle square place the Sea of Galilee, and at the center of its right edge Lake Huleh. Continue Jordan River southward in middle square, and place Dead Sea in upper right-hand of lower-center square. Then mark the zones on the map in colors, searching the chapters forward to find their limits. Use crayons or water colors.

2. Mark on First Zone, and print names of all cities, places, mountains, and rivers mentioned in the lesson.

3. Make a list, from west to east, and from north to south, of these same places, and write opposite each name the event in Bible history connected with it, and in a third column the Bible reference. Do not fail to look up always the Bible reference and read the passage over.

4. Do the same (as under 2 and 3) for each division of the Second and of the Third Zones.

CHAPTER III

THE THIRD ZONE OF PALESTINE. SAMARIA

Beyond the Plain of Esdraelon, we come to the second division of this Third Zone of the Central Plateau, i.e. SAMARIA. As we pass southward we enter a land of fruitful valleys and rounded hills, covered to their tops with trees and fields, and well-watered by copious springs. The influence of this physical environment upon the inhabitants is most clearly marked. They became a pleasure-loving people, eager for ease and enjoyment, running after idols and wealth, making alliances with powerful nations that might enrich or protect them. Thus Samaria became a buffer-state, between the northern and the southern nations. Egypt and Judea on the south used it as a huge battlefield when in conflict with Syria, Assyria, Persia, etc., on the north. Samaria consequently always suffered.

See opp. p. 11 As we pass below *Bethel,* the landscape becomes more grim, the valleys narrower, more rocks appear, and stern Judea, the land of the shepherd, in contrast to Samaria, the haven of the farmer, lies before us. Judea spelt a desperate struggle, and it alone could produce men of courage and deep intensity, such as Isaiah, Amos, and the like. The real stamina of all Palestine was developed and nourished in this southern section of the wild Judean plateau. Let us traverse Samaria and Judea in detail.

See opp. p. 14 *Samaria* of the New Testament was always *Mount Ephraim* of the Old. Here Ephraim, half of Manasseh, and the tribe of Dan dwelt. Many of the greatest events of Bible history occurred within its borders. After the captivity of the Northern Kingdom of Israel it was filled by foreign peoples sent in by the Assyrians and Babylonians. At Christ's coming, "the Jews had no dealings with the Samaritans," regarding them and their land as polluted. Samaria stretched from the edge of Esdraelon on the north to below Bethel on the south, and from the Jordan to the Plain of Sharon. Although only about twenty-five miles in length, the Jews were so averse to passing through it that they usually crossed the Jordan at the Beth-shan Fords and recrossed at Jericho, in journeying from Galilee to Judea.

Samaria has an average elevation of about 2,000 feet above sea-level, being not so much a mountain mass as a series of high ridges, with plains and elevated valleys between. The slope on the west, towards the Maritime Plain, is gradual; while that on the east to the Jordan River is exceedingly steep and precipitous. In the southern part, it rises 2,800 feet in only nine miles. The chief mountains of Samaria are Mounts Carmel, Gilboa, Ebal, Gerizim and Baal-Hazor. *Mount Carmel* is a ridge rather than a single mountain, just as are Mt. Hermon and Mt. Lebanon. It runs in from the only cape or promontory of the sea-coast, below Phoenicia, with the River Kishon at its base, in a general direction midway between the foot of the Sea of Galilee and the head of the Dead Sea. It is about 12 miles long. At the south-eastern end, where it slopes out into low hills, lies the rich *Valley of Dothan,* in which Joseph found his brethren tend- See opp. p. 14 ing their flocks the day they sold him as a slave. (Gen. 37 : 17.) The Carmel range is of limestone, honeycombed with long, winding caves. Carmel means "Park," and in the Hebrew it is usually "The Park." (See Isa. 35 : 2; Cant. 7 : 5; Amos 1 : 2.) The mountains became a sanctuary or holy spot, in which worship was offered both to Jehovah and to idols. (1 Kings 18 : 19.) *Mount Gilboa* is a barren peak, See opp. p. 14 1,700 feet high, running as a ridge along ten miles, edging the southern border of the Plain of Esdraelon. Here occurred the defeat and death of Saul and Jonathan. (2 Sam. 1 : 17-27.) Here too Gideon gathered his little army of the faithful three hundred. (Judg. 6-8.) *Mount Ebal and Mount Gerizim* lie about the center of Samaria, Ebal (mount of cursing) lay northward; while Gerizim (mount of blessing) lay southward, with the bases not more than a quarter of a mile apart. *The valley and city of Shechem* lay between See opp. p. 14

them. Ebal is 3,076 feet high; Gerizim is 2,848; while the valley is 1,672 feet. Into this valley, Joshua led the entire assemblage of Israelites after the crossing of the Jordan. All came, men, women, and children. The Levites stood in the Valley, with the tribes, half-and-half on the mountains on either side. The Levites read the curses of the law on sin, the tribes on Ebal replied in answer "Amen." They then read the blessings of the law on virtue, and the tribes on Gerizim replied "Amen." Later on, before his death, Joshua again gathered the people here, to listen to his parting counsels. (See Deut. 27; Josh. 8, 24.) Some years later, Jotham (Judg. 9) told the men of Shechem his parable of the trees choosing a king, speaking from a bluff near by, and then ran away to escape their anger. In the period of the restoration of Jerusalem, after the exile, the Samaritans were rejected from participation in the worship of the Temple at Jerusalem. They then set up a temple on Mount Gerizim. When Christ met the woman of Samaria, she spoke to Him of that worship, saying "Our fathers worshipped in this mountain." (S. John 4 : 20.) That temple however had been destroyed 170 years before. Shechem has had many names. Its present name is *Nablous.* It is also practically the site of See opp. p. 15 *Sychar,* where Jacob's Well stands, and where our Lord met the Samaritan Woman, referred to above. It has been the common opinion that Shechem and Sychar were the same; but much recent research seems to indicate that they were two separate towns, Sychar being about two miles to the southeast of Shechem. Sychar has been identified with Askar, at the base of Mount Ebal. The Samaritan name Shechem closely resembled Sychar, and the two were confounded by the Crusaders, so that Shechem was said to be Sychar. Explorations have made the situation of Jacob's Well one of the most assured spots in Palestine, and located Askar and Sychar as identical. The proximity of the two towns however makes them practically one situation. At Shechem, Abimelech, the usurper, set up his brief kingdom. Another usurper, Jeroboam, the son of Nebat, was crowned here by the Ten Tribes. (1 Kings 12 : 25.) Another name seems to have been *Neapolis,* in the Grecian Period. In the early

MODERN SAMARIA

PLAIN OF DOTHAN
Copyrighted by Underwood & Underwood

BATTLEFIELD OF GIDEON
Copyrighted by Underwood & Underwood

SHECHEM
Copyrighted by Underwood & Underwood

SYCHAR

JACOB'S WELL

JEZREEL
Photo by S. U. Mitman

RAMAH

dawn of the history of Israel, Abram, coming across the
Jordan, built his first altar to God, and rested in Shechem.
(Gen. 12 : 7.) Before the exodus was completed by the
conquest of Canaan, the people regarded it as holy. (Deut.
11 : 29; Josh. 24 : 32.) Near it were *Joseph's Tomb* (Gen.
33 : 19; S. John 4 : 6) and *Jacob's Well.* *Baal-Hazor,* twenty See opp. p. 15
miles south of Gerizim, five miles north of Bethel, is the
highest mountain of Samaria, 3,300 feet. On its slope Absalom had his sheep-shearing farm, where at a great feast he
had summoned, he treacherously killed his brother Amnon.
(2 Sam. 13 : 2-29.)

Among other cities to be considered is *Jezreel,* seated on a See o. p. p. 15
foothill of Mount Gilboa. It commanded a vista over the
entire valley of Jezreel. (2 Kings 9 : 17.) Ahab and Jezebel
made it their capital, when that wicked king reigned in Israel. His royal palace stood on the eastern wall of the
city, and from its window Jezebel was cast down to the
hungry dogs below, in the open space where the city refuse
was thrown. (2 Kings 9 : 30-35; 1 Kings 21 : 1.) The
vineyard of Naboth was hard by the palace. The modern
name is *Zerin,* though only a collection of ruined huts remains. *Tirzah* is another city of this region, probably near
Shechem, though its site is not yet definitely fixed. It was
noted for its beauty and was, at one time, the second royal
city. Zimri was besieged there, and to avoid capture, set
fire to his palace and was burned himself. (Song of Sol.
6 : 4; 1 Kings 14 : 17; 15 : 33; 16 : 18.) Six miles northwest of Shechem and twenty-three miles from the sea-
coast, lies the *Mount or Hill of Samaria,* standing isolated
and alone in the midst of a wide green basin. King Omri,
the father of Ahab, bought it of Shemer, its owner, for two
talents of silver. From the name of its owner, Omri gave the
town the title of Shomeron, which became altered to Samaria.
From that time on it was the capital of the Northern Kingdom of Israel. The city was almost impregnable. It with-
stood two severe sieges, 901 and 910 B. C., and Shalmaneser
finally took three years to capture it. (1 Kings 20 : 1; 2
Kings 6 : 24-27 : 20; 18 : 9, 10.) Under Ahab and Jezebel, it
became the center for an ornate idolatrous worship, in its most

licentious forms. (Isa. 28 : 1-4.) Near the time of Christ
it was rebuilt by King Herod, and named *Sebaste,* the Greek
of Augustus, equivalent to Augusta. The colonnades and pil-
lars of Herod, all in ruins, still remain standing, as a mute
witness to the city's pristine grandeur. The old name clung
to it, and it was known in Christ's time as Samaria. S. Philip
preached with great success in the city in its power, "there
was great joy in the city." (Acts 8 : 5-8.) The ruins
of the Church of St. John the Baptist, built by the Crusaders, still stand upon the slope of the hill, erected in
the twelfth century. It ran more than 3,000 feet with
its sweeping colonnade. The remains of an old reservoir,
the *Pool of Samaria,* are also to be seen, where was once
washed the blood-stained chariot of Ahab, when the infamous
king met his doom. (1 Kings 22 : 38.) Well indeed has the
prophecy of Micah the prophet been literally fulfilled. (Micah
1 : 1-6.)

Shiloh, now called *Seilun,* lies in a secluded valley, twelve
miles southeast of Shechem, nine miles north of Bethel. Its
site is definitely named in Judges 21 : 19. Its ruins have
been positively identified.

For about 400 years, in the period of the Judges, Shiloh
was the seat of the tabernacle worship, and the Ark of the
Covenant was kept here. It was the most esteemed sanctuary
of the whole land. (Josh. 18; Judg. 21 : 19.) In later
years the ark was lost to Shiloh through its capture by the
Philistines. (1 Sam. 4.) When the tribe of Benjamin had
been all but exterminated by the other tribes, the men
repaired to Shiloh and captured the young women of the
town, to be their wives, and so rehabilitate the tribe. (Judg.
21 : 19-23.)

At SHILOH, Joshua completed the division of the land
among the tribes. (Josh. 18 : 6.) Here Eli ministered as
high priest, and Samuel grew up as a child. At Shiloh lived
the prophet Ahijah, whom the wife of Jeroboam came to
visit, concerning the life of her sick son. (1 Kings 14 : 2.)
Gilgal, seven miles north of Bethel, should be distinguished
from the Gilgal near Jericho, where Israel encamped after
crossing the Jordan. This northern Gilgal is the place where

Samuel set up a school of the prophets, from which Elijah went to Bethel, and then on to Jericho, on his last visit to the "sons of the prophets." (2 Kings 2 : 1; 4 : 38.)

Besides the rivers flowing into the Mediterranean, which take their rise in the mountains of Ephraim or Samaria, all of which we have studied under the Maritime Plain, we have one river of Bible mention, flowing eastward into the Jordan, *the Farah*. It rises at the base of Mount Ebal. It is "the waters of Ænon," mentioned by S. John. (S. John 3 : 23.)

Questions and Manual Work on Chapter III.

1. What Old Testament events are connected with the places of the Maritime Plain? the Plain of Sharon? Philistia?

2. What Old Testament events are connected with localities in the Shephelah? In Galilee?

3. What New Testament events, if any, are connected with these several divisions?

4. Draw an outline map of the region of Samaria, alone, making it on a scale at least four inches across. On it locate the places, mountains, rivers, etc., in proper order, by dot and name.

5. Make a list, as in previous chapter, of places in order of events and Bible references.

CHAPTER IV

The third great division, southward, of the Third Zone, that of the Central Plateau, is JUDEA, that portion of Canaan which in the settlement of the land was assigned by Joshua to the tribes of Benjamin, Judah, Simeon, and Dan. Judah and Benjamin were the most important, and the former, in fact, the chief ruling tribe of all. Simeon seems to have had part of the dry South Land or Negeb, next the desert. Dan was west of Benjamin, between the valleys of Aijalon and Sorek. (Josh. 15-19.) All this territory became practically the kingdom of Judah, the southern kingdom, after the division ensuing upon Solomon's death. It was called the Kingdom of Judah. After the return from exile it became Judea and its inhabitants Jews. The exceedingly mountainous character of this part of Palestine has ever made the sturdy nature of this people. Every nation and tribe that dwelt there developed hardihood and courage, high principles and noble morals. For many centuries, the inhabitants kept very much to themselves, hemmed in by rocky walls. They took no part in the wars of Gideon and Barak, and held aloof from either progress, conquest, or commerce. Yet this very isolation enabled Judea to hold out against the great world powers, Babylon, Assyria, Egypt, Rome, for a century and a half after the Northern Kingdom was extinct. The entire size of this territory was but thirty miles wide, from the Jordan to the Philistine Plain, and fifty-five miles long, from Geba to Beersheba, 1,500 square miles in all (see 2 Kings 23 : 8), less than half as large as the State of Rhode Island. Judea has always been a land of shepherds, although as a whole it is a rocky, barren, rugged land—mountains, wilderness, stones everywhere—and in the southern extremity, wild, desolate, and uninviting. It is also an unusually dry section. In the whole length and breadth there are not more than six or seven streams that have water the entire year. Scanning the country in detail, from the north downwards, as we did the other sections, we would locate two towns by name, for their sites are uncertain, just below Gilgal, our last town in the Middle Section, Samaria. One of these towns is *Gophna,* probably the modern village of Jufna, the most northerly on the western plateau of Judea. It was called *Ophni* at the time of the conquest. (Josh. 18 : 24.) It was the last halting-place of Titus on his ill-fated march to Jerusalem. *Ophrah,* the second, was a frontier town on the northeast corner, thirteen miles north of Jerusalem. It has been identified with *Ephron or Ephraim,* mentioned in 2 Chron. 13 : 19 and S. John 11 : 54, where Christ rested from the throng, after the raising of Lazarus.

Bethel, "the house of God," modern *Beitin,* is on the main road, ten miles north of Jerusalem, seven south of Gilgal. The ridge of mountain on which the ruins of the ancient city still stand, is almost 2,900 feet above the sea. There are now, says Dr. Schaff, "about two dozen Moslem hovels, the ruins of a Greek church, a very large cistern, and wild rocks." Scarcely any spot in all the Holy Land has so many events gathered around it. Abraham first rested here on his journey south from Shechem. (Gen. 12 : 8.) Here Lot surveyed the land and selected his future residence. (Gen. 13 : 1-10.) Here Jacob in his flight rested on a stone and dreamed his vision of angels. (Gen. 28 : 10-22.) It was one of Samuel's sacred sanctuaries. (Judg. 20 : 18, 26-28; 21 : 4; 1 Sam. 7 : 16.) Jeroboam made it a city of idol worship. (1 Kings 12 : 27-29, 32, 33; 13 : 1-10.) Part of the time it was held by the Northern Kingdom and part by the Southern. (See Picture 15.) *Ai* or *Hai,* mentioned in Joshua 8, is probably the heap of ruins two miles east of Bethel. *Rock Rimmon,* a small village four miles east of Bethel on the edge of the plateau on the side of a mountain sloping down to the great ravine filled with numberless caves is the spot to which the survivors of the tribe of Benjamin fled after the battles noted in Judges 20 : 28-47. *Michmash (Mukmas)* has

been placed at the modern village four miles southeast of
Bethel. The rocky gorge up which Jonathan climbed and the
spot from which he began his perilous descent (1 Sam. 14 :
13) are both seen here. The Philistines had come to Michmash
by way of the Valley of Aijalon, while the handful of soldiers
belonging to Saul were encamped at *Gibeah,* on the other
side of the gorge. The bravery of Jonathan and his armor-
bearer saved the day for Israel. Here, too, Joshua had
fought, in aid of his allies the Gibeonites. (Josh. 10 : 1-14.)
Michmash was also on the route of the Assyrians, as they
marched south, noted in Isaiah 10 : 28. After the exile the
remnant of the tribe of Benjamin reoccupied the spot.
(Neh. 11 : 31.) *Geba* or *Jeba* was on the south side of this
same chasm, and at the time of Josiah was the frontier town
of Judah. (2 Kings 23 : 8.) It was also again inhabited
after the exile. *Ramah of Benjamin,* six miles south of
Bethel, is one of the many Ramahs (high places) of the
Old Testament, where sacrifices were offered. It is mentioned several times in the Bible, but not with any very
special event. (Look up 1 Kings 15 : 17, 22; Josh. 18 : 25;
Judg. 4 : 5.) It is not the Ramah where Samuel was born.
See opp. p. 15 (1 Sam. 1 : 1.) *Gibeah of Benjamin,* also known as Gibeah
of Saul, may be the same as Geba; but is most likely to be
the name of a general district, including Geba and Gibeon,
on the edge of the plateau. Here occurred the almost total
destruction of Benjamin. (Judg. 19 and 20.) Here also
was the lonely watch of Rizpah, the mother of the two
young men hanged here. (2 Sam. 21 : 1-14.) *Gibeon* is to
the west of Geba, on a hill about six miles from Jerusalem.
At the foot of this hill is the *Pool of Gibeon,* where the
hosts of Abner and Joab met in battle. (2 Sam. 2 : 13.)
It was the chief Hivite city that surrendered to Joshua. At
this spot was fought the great battle of the Amorite Confederacy, which decided its fate, when the Amorites were
driven headlong down the steep Beth-horon Pass. Read the
thrilling account in Joshua 10 : 10, 11. At the great Stone
of Gibeon Amasa was slain, and at the same spot, years
later, his murderer, Joab, met his punishment by death at
the hand of Benaiah, Solomon's captain. (2 Sam. 20 : 10;

1 Kings 2 : 29-34.) At Gibeon the Tabernacle was set up after Saul slew the priests; and on the brazen altar in front of the Tabernacle, Solomon offered a thousand burnt-offerings, and here this same king made the choice of wisdom, above all other rewards. (Josh. 9 : 3-15; 2 Sam. 20 : 8; 1 Kings 3 : 4.) Just south of Gibeon is *Mizpah*, but five miles northwest of Jerusalem. It is the highest point on the plateau, nearly 3,000 feet. Mizpah is identified as the Watch-Tower of Benjamin. It was the center to which the people gathered to consult regarding the rebellion of Benjamin (Judg. 20 : 1-11) ; and again to offer sacrifices (1. Sam. 7 : 5) and to elect Saul their king. (1 Sam. 10 : 17.) It was also one of the three Judgment Cities of Samuel. (1 Sam. 7 : 16.) Gedaliah was killed here with his few followers around him. (2 Kings 25 : 22-25; Jer. 41 : 1-8.) *Nob,* a priestly city, lies near by to the east, though its site is somewhat uncertain. (1 Sam. 21 : 1; 22 : 9.) Still eastward is *Anathoth,* three miles northeast of Jerusalem, a Levitical town (Josh. 21 : 18), to which Abiathar was banished (1 Kings 2 : 26), and the birthplace of Jeremiah the prophet. (Jer. 1 : 1.)

Questions and Manual Work on Chapter IV.

1. What do you consider the four chief localities and events of the First Zone of Palestine? Of the Second?

2. What are the Divisions of the Third Zone?

3. What are the chief localities of Galilee? Of Samaria?

4. What territory did the third division of the Third Zone cover?

5. What is the chief physical characteristic of this region? How did it affect the character of the inhabitants?

6. Draw on the general map the places mentioned.

7. Make a list of the events connected with them, and a column of the Bible references.

CHAPTER V

JERUSALEM AND ITS ENVIRONS

See opp. p. 24 We are now approaching the great city of all Palestine; indeed, the most sacred city of all the world, *Jerusalem*, passing out of the country assigned to Benjamin into that belonging to the tribe of Judah. We shall consider certain mountains, rivers, and cities, in direct relation to this capital of the Southern Kingdom, in order to fix them in mind more readily.

Jerusalem is situated, roughly speaking, about one-third of the way across the head of the Dead Sea, towards the Mediterranean Sea. To be exact, it is on a mountain tableland, 2,500 feet above the Great Sea and 3,800 feet above the Dead Sea, thirty miles from the former and eighteen miles from the latter. Ravines and gorges surround the city on every side, save the north. *The Valley of Jehoshaphat,* in which the River Kidron flows, is to the east, separating the town from the Mount of Olives. The western valley is the *Valley of Hinnom*. It separates Jerusalem from the *Hill of Evil Counsel,* where the plot to betray Christ was hatched, at the base of which is the *Potter's Field, Aceldama or the Field of Blood,* bought with the price of Judas' betrayal of our Lord. The lower part of the Valley of Hinnom was called *Tophet* or the Place of Fire or *Gehenna,* and was used as a place for burning the refuse of the great city above. Let us now examine more closely some of these surrounding features, before studying the city. *The Mount of Olives* is a curved ridge, 2,637 feet high, to the east of Jerusalem. It was along this route that David passed when he fled from See opp. p. 24 Absalom. (2 Sam. 15 : 23, 30.) Here, in *the Garden of Gethsemane,* on its western slope, near Jerusalem, the Agony of our Blessed Lord took place. (S. Matt. 26; S. Mark 14; S.

22

Luke 24; Acts 1 : 12.) Two small mountain torrents, practically not more than winter streams, flow from this western
mountain region, to the North, and empty South toward the
Dead Sea. One is the *Brook Cherith*, probably the present See opp. p. 24
Wady Kelt, near Jericho. It was by this brook that Elijah hid
from Ahab, and in his solitude was fed by God's ministrations.
(1 Kings 17 : 3.) The second stream, *the Kidron,* flows
through the Valley of Jehoshaphat, along the eastern side of
the City of Jerusalem, between it and the Mount of Olives.

Flowing southeasterly, it passes Bethlehem and runs through
the crags and wilderness of Judea, ending with a dash over
the rough rocks on the shore of the Dead Sea. The valley
is referred to by Joel (Joel 3 : 2, 12) and is called elsewhere the King's Dale. (Gen. 14 : 17; 2 Sam. 18 : 18.)
Rubbish to the depth of 70 or 80 feet has accumulated in this
valley, and the original bed of the river has moved eastward
as much as 70 feet, on account of the huge piles of débris
that have poured down from the heights above. The Brook
Kidron is mentioned often in Bible history. Over it the
bridge crossed into the City of cities, and this bridge formed
part of the path the Master and His Disciples trod each time
they entered the Sacred City. Ezekiel's Vision pictures it,
through his creative power, as a spiritual river, rising in a
tiny stream from beneath the Temple and flowing, with ever-
growing volume and power, until it empties as a mighty
torrent into the sea below. This, of course, was imaginative;
but the symbolism of divine grace, to which it was applied,
is forceful. (Ezek. 47 : 1-12.) *The Wilderness of Judea,*
through which this river flows, called often the *Jeshimon,* is
a long, narrow district, 10 miles wide by 35 miles long,
lying on the western side of the Dead Sea. It is formed of
plains of barren limestone rock, which mountain streams
have furrowed with deep channels. It is a barren, desolate
region, until the rainy season sets in, when, for a brief
period, the "desert rejoices, and blossoms as the rose."
(Isa. 35 : 1.) Somewhere in this wilderness was the cave
where David cut off Saul's robe (1 Sam. 24 : 1-22) and
where our Lord was tempted by Satan. (S. Matt. 3 : 1 to 4 : 1.)
About twelve miles from Jerusalem, along the dreary gorge

of the Kidron, on high rocks on the very edge of the gorge,
stands the famous *Monastery of Mar Saba*, of the Greek
Church, founded in the fifth century by S. Saba.   There are
only about 60 monks there now, though at one time it was
filled with an assemblage of unusual men.   Half way down
this Wilderness of Jeshimon, the sea edge of the desert, is a
fertile and wonderful oasis, called *En-gedi,* half a mile
square, filled with delightful fruits and vineyards, made so
by being in a hollow 400 feet lower than the surrounding
plain, and so nourished with abundant water.   (See Song of
Solomon 1 : 14.)   It is called to-day *Ain Jidy.*   The old Bible
name was *Hazazon-tamar, or Hazazon of the Palm.*   (Gen.
14 : 7; 2 Chron. 20 : 2.)   Through the Pass of En-gedi, from
the rugged plateau above, the hosts of Ammon and Moab
climbed up from the Dead Sea and entered that plain near
Tekoa, known as the ascent of *Ziz.*   (2 Chron. 20 : 16-20.)
A few miles south of En-gedi, back of the desert, about half-
way between En-gedi and the lower end of the Dead Sea,
stands *Masada,* which was the last refuge of the Jews after
the destruction of Jerusalem by Titus (70 A. D.).   It is one
of the strongest natural fortresses in all the world, 1,300 feet
higher than the surrounding land, and can be reached only
by men in single file, climbing a narrow, step-cut rock.   The
Maccabees first made a fortress of this rock.   Herod the
Great fled there in danger.

See opp. p. 24   Returning to the country immediately around Jerusalem,
we note *Bethany,* on the road to Jericho, near the Kidron,
two miles from Jerusalem, on the Mount of Olives.   It was
and is but a small village.   Here lived S. Mary and S. Martha ;
here Christ raised Lazarus, their brother, from the dead ;
and here he often sojourned with the trio, and spent the last
few nights previous to the Crucifixion.   (S. John 11 : 1-44;
S. Matt. 21 : 17; S. Mark 11 : 12, 19.)   The site of *Bethphage.*
mentioned in connection with the Palm Sunday entry, is not
definitely known, but is, of course, between Bethany and the
Mount of Olives.

We come now to the study of *Jerusalem* itself.   The city
has been known by a different name in each great period
of its checkered history.   In the Patriarchal time, as the seat

JERUSALEM

GARDEN OF GETHSEMANE

BROOK CHERITH

BETHANY

TOWER OF DAVID
Jerusalem

LANE LEADING TO HEROD'S
PALACE

POOL OF HEZEKIAH

CHURCH OF THE HOLY
SEPULCHRE
Exterior

of Melchizedek's priestly kingdom, it was called *Salem,* pronounced Shalem. (Gen. 14 : 18; Psa. 76 : 2.) During the Jebusite period it was known as *Jebus.* (Judg. 19 : 10.) After its capture by David, the first time it was held by the Israelites, *Jerusalem,* properly *Jeru-shalaim.* It is first mentioned thus in Judges 1 : 7, 8, where it may have come by euphony from *Jebus-shalem.* It means thus "possession of peace." It was called by the prophets by the poetic name *Ariel,* "the lion of God" (Isa. 29 : 1), and in S. Matt. 4 : 5, 27 : 53, the *"Holy City."* After it was destroyed by Titus (70 A. D.) it was rebuilt by the emperor Aelius Hadrianus, A. D. 135, and named *Aelia Capitolina,* a name it held till 536 A. D., when it resumed its old name, Jerusalem. It is now named by the Arabs, *El Khuds esh-Sherif,* "the Holy City," shortened to *El Khuds.*

We would recall that the *Valley of Jehoshaphat,* through which the Kidron flows, runs around the east and southeast; the *Valley of Hinnom* (Josh. 15 : 8) around the south and southwest, joining the former valley at Siloam, which we shall study later; and the *Valley of Gihon* (1 Kings 1 : 33) completes the western side, though some place this in the lower part of the Kidron Valley. A shallow valley, *the Tyropoeon,* shaped like a new moon, runs through the city itself, dividing the lower part into two hills. The entire city is composed of four hills. Towards the southwest, between the Tyropoeon and the Valley of Hinnom, was *Mount Zion,* 2,540 feet high. It was the highest of the hills and the one on which most of the city was built in Christ's time. On it stood the old Jebusite fortress, which was at last captured by David. Zion was known as the Upper City and also as the City of David. (2 Sam. 5 : 7-9; 1 Chron. 11 : 4-7.) *The Palace of Herod,* Agrippa's Palace, and David's Tomb were all on this mountain. Most of this portion is now the Armenian Quarter. *The Armenian Convent,* the largest modern building in Jerusalem; the *English Church,* the *Church of St. James,* and the *Environments of the Holy Sepulchre* are all in this quarter. On the northwest hill is Acra, 2,490 feet high, known as the Lower City, the Christian Quarter. In the lower southwest corner of this quarter is See opp. p. 25 See opp. p. 25

See opp. p. 25 the *Pool of Hezekiah,* a large reservoir with a capacity of nearly three million gallons. It is supposed to be the "pool and conduit" constructed by Hezekiah to bring water to the city. (2 Kings 20 : 20.) The water comes through the conduit from the Mamilla Pool, far up in the Valley of Hinnom.

See opp. p. 25 The *Church of the Holy Sepulchre* is almost in the center of this quarter, and is really a collection of several churches and chapels. It seems to be proved without much doubt that it is not the actual locality of the burial-place of our See opp. p. 28 Lord, for a great many satisfactory reasons. It could not have stood without the second great wall of the city, without a formation in the wall-line that would have been ridiculous. The tomb is unlike the hundreds of rock-hewn tombs all around that locality and does not agree with the Bible story, and the accumulation of a large number of other impossible sites fixed around it, for manifest convenience, all tend to discredit in every way this as the true spot. As this site, with this church and a former one, has been the same since the days of Constantine, it would seem that we do not know just where the real tomb was. Perhaps this is wisely so, since God has apparently intended that none of the materials of sacred story should come down to man for superstitious veneration and perhaps idolatry. *The Moslem (Mohammedan) Quarter* lies northeast, and is the largest division of the modern city. Here are located the *Governor's Palace,* the *Church of S. Anne,* the *Pool of Bethesda,* and the *Via* See opp. p. 28 *Dolorosa*. In the wall of this quarter is *S. Stephen's Gate,* through which S. Stephen is supposed to have passed on the See opp. p. 28 way to his fateful stoning.* *The Pool of Bethesda* has been recently excavated, near the Church of S. Anne, with a flight of twenty-four stone steps leading down to it, and supporting arches and porches along the sides. The Crusaders built a church over the pool, and a fresco on the wall of the crypt shows an angel troubling the water, a manifest indication that they were certain of the right site. The Via Dolorosa, along which our Blessed Lord is supposed to have passed on the way to Calvary, runs from the Governor's Palace to the Church of the Holy Sepulchre, as we have it placed to-day. Under the rock surface of the northern part of this section

* Many state that the Damascus Gate is really the one through which St. Stephen passed, but Hurlbut prefers St. Stephen's Gate.

lie the *Royal Quarries,* from which the huge stones used in the construction of Solomon's Temple were undoubtedly cut.

Questions and Manual Work on Chapter V.

1. Transfer localities noted on special map of Samaria to the general map you are making.

2. Get an outline map of Jerusalem (Bailey Series, S. S. Commission) and locate carefully, with dot and name, (a) the chief places *outside* the city walls. (b) the four divisions of the city itself, and the sites mentioned in the first three of them.

3. Make a list of places and events, as in previous Chapters, with Bible reference for each.

4. If time, try to mold a relief map in sand, clay or plasticine of the city and its valleys.

CHAPTER VI

JERUSALEM, CONTINUED. FOURTH QUARTER AND SURROUNDING ROADS

The last Quarter of Jerusalem lies to the southeast, between the Tyropoeon Valley and the Kidron Valley. It is *Mount Moriah*. On the northern corner is the site of the Temple and the southern section was known as the *Hill Ophel*. It is to-day the *Jewish Quarter*. It contains several Synagogues; but has no large buildings. Its streets are dark and narrow, densely populated, with buildings close together. Over the Temple Area, originally a sharp-pointed rock rising many feet above the surrounding land, but later made level by a wall 70 feet high, filled in with stones and earth, is a raised platform of almost five acres, paved with white marble. The original rock rises through this platform fifteen feet high. Tradition says that here Abraham sought to sacrifice Isaac; later it was the *Threshing Floor of Araunah* (1 Chron. 21 : 20; 2 Sam. 24 : 18-20); and still later the site of the Holy of Holies of the Temple.* On this sacred spot have stood the Temples of Solomon, 1,000 B. C.; of Nehemiah (2 Chron. 3 : 1), often known as the Temple of Zerubbabel (586 B. C.); the Temple of Herod (time of Christ); and is now occupied by the wonderful structure, the fane of the Mohammedans, the most beautiful building in Jerusalem, See opp. p. 28 the octagonal *Dome of the Rock*, often but wrongly called the Mosque of Omar. Next after Mecca it is to the Moslems the most sacred spot in all the world, and "after Cordova, the most beautiful in any land." From the great wall to the west ran a bridge spanning the Tyropoeon, one of the remains of the arches discovered about 1850 by Dr. Robinson. and See opp. p. 29 named after him, *Robinson's Arch. The Wailing Place of the Jews,* gigantic stones of the wall on the eastern boundary of

---

* It is disputed whether the "Holy of Holies" or the "Altar of Burnt Offering" is found here. Calkin, Stewart, Hurlbut, and Tarbell lean towards the "Holy of Holies."

CHURCH OF THE HOLY
SEPULCHRE
Interior

ARCH OF ECCE HOMO

OLD RUINS OF THE POOL
OF BETHESDA

MOSQUE OF OMAR

WAILING PLACE OF THE JEWS
Wall of the Temple

GOLGOTHA

S. STEPHEN'S GATE

POOL OF SILOAM

the Quarter, is the place of weekly assemblage of the Hebrews, who weep over the lost glory of the Sacred City. The Place of the Crucifixion of our Lord, *Calvary,* is pretty See opp. p. 29 definitely settled in a rounded knob or hill, outside the *Damascus Gate* (the shape of a skull), north of the Mohammedan See opp. p. 29 Quarter, not far from the Grotto of Jeremiah, outside the City Wall.* The water supply of Jerusalem came partly from natural springs and partly from reservoirs collecting rain water. *The Pool of Siloam* lies on the southeast of the city See opp. p. 29 in the Valley of Jehoshaphat (Kidron) near the mouth of the Tyropoeon Valley. It received intermittent supplies of water from a spring on the northeast of the city, brought down by a long underground aqueduct. *Tophet, or Gehenna,* was a name for the lower basin of the Valley of Hinnom. Here were practised the awful rites of Moloch, and, later on, it was used as a place in which to burn the offal of the great city, so that a perpetual fire and smoke arose, and its name naturally became a synonym for the Place of Punishment. (See 2 Kings 23 : 10; Isa. 30 : 33; 66 : 24; Jer. 19 : 6, etc.) The *Fountain of the Virgin* is the only spring of running water in or about Jerusalem. It issues from a hidden source, under the foot of Mt. Orphel, about 950 feet south of the city gate. It is probably the *"Fountain of Siloam,"* referred to by Josephus, the *En Rogel,* or Spring of the Fuller mentioned frequently in the Old Testament, and the source or headwaters of the Pool of Siloam. The *Village of Siloam* See opp. p. 32 is perched on a lofty cliff, across the Kidron, opposite this Fountain. It is mentioned in S. Luke 13 : 4, in connection with the fall of its tower. The Pool of Siloam at the mouth of the Valley is fed by a long underground aqueduct, recently discovered and explored, from the Fountain above noted. At En Rogel, Adonijah held his feast. (1 Kings 1 : 19.) Solomon was anointed by the Pool of Siloam (1 Kings 1 : 38-46.) The canal or rock-hewn aqueduct is 67 feet long, so that the distance is not very great from these several sites. (See also Josh. 15 : 7; 18 : 16; 2 Sam. 17 : 17.) The Fountain was probably *the Upper Gihon* and the Pool *the Lower Gihon.* (See 2 Chron. 32 : 30; Isa. 7 : 3.) The recently recovered Pool is surrounded by massive stone steps,

---

* Stewart, Tarbell and Kent favor this site. There are three views as to the place of the Crucifixion: 1. Here. 2. The Church of the Holy Sepulchre. 3. A site further away from the City. In the main, Gordon's Calvary is accepted today.

recalling Nehemiah 3 : 15 and the descent of the Blind Man.
(S. John 9 : 7.)   It was the Pool from which the golden
pitcher of water was brought on the last, great day of the
Feast of Tabernacles. (S. John 7 : 37.)

Having thus explored Jerusalem and its immediate environs, let us glance back at the City of cities, e'er we follow
and examine the six chief roads leading from its portals. It
was an almost impregnable city in Bible times, particularly
in the period of the Old Testament. Encircling ravines,
much deeper then than now, surrounded it on three sides.
On the east, south, and west, it was practically unassailable,
owing to the combined natural ravine-defenses and the walls
erected above them. On the north there is no natural break
between the City and the surrounding plateau. Before the
siege of Titus (A. D. 70), this quarter was protected by
three massive rows of walls, at some distance from each
other, with towers and deep moats or ditches. Each time
these walls were broken down by enemies they were rebuilt,
not always precisely in the same spot however, so that iden-
tification of the old lines to-day, for certain periods, is somewhat doubtful. Thus the Jebusites were able to hold it a long
period, and even sent a mocking defiance to David. (2 Sam.
5 : 6.)

Six roads diverge from the Sacred City in as many directions. We shall note them and follow several to important
neighboring towns. *The Northern Road* starts from the
Damascus Gate and runs straight north, through Shechem to
Damascus. All the important towns along this route have
been visited by us in our previous chapters. *The Eastern
Road* traverses the region of crags and caves of robbers
which have ever frequented its pathway since the days of
the Good Samaritan, the road leading down to Jericho, a
continuous descent from 2,700 feet above the Sea to 1,300
feet below it in a distance of but twenty miles. It is the road

See opp. p. 32 around the *Mount of Olives* to Bethany, on its slope. *The
Southern Road* follows the crest of hills to Hebron. On it
are several important sites not yet considered. Just south
of the City is the *Plain of Rephaim,* where David twice over-
came the Philistines, after the capture of Jerusalem. (2 Sam.

5 : 18-25.)   Six miles southeast of Jerusalem, on this road, is *Bethlehem,* one of the three most important cities in all the See opp. p. 32 world, Jerusalem and Nazareth being the other two.   Here See opp. p. 32 lived Jesse and David, and here was born the great Son of David, Christ our Lord.   It stands on the side and summit of a steep hill, and to-day has about 8,000 inhabitants.   In a cave near this village, Jerome wrote his Vulgate translation See opp. p. 33 of the Holy Bible, the standard version of the Roman Church, The old name of the town was *Ephrath.*   About a mile from the town is shown *Rachel's tomb.*   (Gen. 48 : 7.)   Bethlehem was the home of Boaz, the site of the exquisite story of Ruth and Naomi.   (See Ruth.   Also S. Luke 2 : 4-14.)   Just a little beyond Bethlehem lies the *Valley of Elah,* in which David fought with Goliath of Gath, leader of the Philistines. (1 Sam. 17.)   Passing on through the Jeshimon, or "the Waste," the desolate region south, the Wilderness of Judea in which lay *the Mount of the Temptation*, we come to *He-* See opp. p. 33 *bron,* eighteen miles below Jerusalem, one of the most ancient towns in the world, occupied before the days of Abraham.   In the Bible, it is called the *Vale of Hebron* (Gen. 37 : 14), and the expanse north of the town is called the *Plain of Mamre.* Hebron was built seven years before the town of Tanis or Zoan in Egypt.   (Num. 13 : 22.)   Abraham dwelt here, the See opp. p. 33 Patriarchs were buried here, Isaac, Jacob, and Joseph called it their home.   (Gen. 37 : 14.)   It was a Hittite city in the time of Abraham and a stronghold later of the Anakim.   At the Conquest it went to Caleb and became a City of Refuge. See opp. p. 33 (Josh. 14 : 10-15.)   David reigned first at Hebron and here Absalom set up his rebellion.   (2 Sam. 5 : 5; 15 : 7-12.)

The Southwestern Road runs from Jerusalem down "to Gaza, which is desert."   (See map.)   (Acts 8 : 26.)   It traverses ravines and deserts and has no towns along the route.   *The Western Road* runs to Joppa on the sea-coast. Four miles or more from the Sacred City it reaches *Emmaus,* recently identified.   This is the town and this the road where the Risen Lord appeared to his two disciples as they journeyed from the Capital the evening of his Resurrection.   (S. Luke 24 : 13.)   *Kirjath-jearim,* where the Ark rested when it was brought from the Philistines at Beth-shemesh lies along this road. (1 Sam. 6 : 21 ; 2 Sam. 6 : 2.) *The Northwestern Road* emerges from the Northern Road just beyond Gibeah, and winds down the hills to Joppa. On it are *Mizpah, Gibeon, and Beth-horon,* all of which we have visited.

One other city only remains to be considered, *Beer-sheba,* which marks the southern limit of the country, far south, on the great highroad between Palestine and Egypt.

It was at various times the home of Abraham, Isaac, and Jacob. Abraham's wells are still there. (Gen. 21 : 31.) It was the center of patriarchal history. Here occurred most of the events mentioned in their lives. (Look up carefully Gen. 21 : 33; 28 : 10; 46 : 1; 22 : 3, 19; 25 : 34; 27 : 23; Josh. 19 : 2; Judg. 20 : 1; 1 Sam. 3 : 20; 1 Sam. 8 : 2.) Hither Elijah fled from the wrath of Jezebel. (1 Kings 19 : 3.) Later it became a seat of idolatrous worship and was severely denounced by God's prophets. (Amos 5 : 5; 8 : 14; 2 Kings 23 : 8.) All this south country, centering at Beer-sheba, was called *the Negeb,* meaning "dry," bordering on the Arabian Desert, a dry, parched land. The nature of the country demanded a nomadic life. Consequently its See opp. p. 36 inhabitants always were a roving people. *Kadesh-Barnea,* still farther south, 48 miles from Beer-sheba, almost out of the Negeb, has been identified recently. *Ain Qadis* or *Ain Quadis* had been located in 1842 and then lost track of, until the present generation. Most of the events in Numbers 13-20 (which see and read) occurred here. *Mount Hor,* where Aaron died and was buried is just above it. (See Deut. 10 : 6 and Num. 20 : 22-28.)

Questions and Manual Work on Chapter VI.

1. Draw from memory a rough outline map of Jerusalem, and locate the surroundings. Make the same on the sand table.

2. Tell or write all you know of the several Temples that have stood on the rock in the Jewish Quarter of Jerusalem.

3. With what localities is the name Siloam connected?

4. Write down the name of each road diverging from the City and tabulate, in order, the chief places and the events and Bible references.

SILOAM VILLAGE

MOUNT OF OLIVES

BETHLEHEM

CHURCH OF THE NATIVITY
Interior

FIELD OF THE SHEPHERDS

HEBRON

MT. OF TEMPTATION

Photo by S. U. Mitman

TOMBS OF THE KINGS

CHAPTER VII

The Fourth great Zone of Palestine, to the east, is the
VALLEY OF THE JORDAN RIVER, a vast depression or
rift, extending north and south, practically the entire length
of the country. The Valley itself is the largest and most
wonderful in the world, extending from the foot of the
Taurus Mountains to the Gulf of Akabah, a distance of 550
miles. There are only three other such tracts comparable to
it, one in Asia, near the Caspian Sea; one in the Sahara in
Africa; and one in southeast California.

In ancient times, the whole of Palestine was undoubtedly
under the ocean. Then came the upheavals, causing mountains on either side, with a fall or fracture forming the
gigantic valley. At the Dead Sea it reaches a depression
of 1,300 feet, the lowest valley in the world. Professor George
Adam Smith well says: "there may be something on the
surface of another planet to match the Jordan Valley,—
there is nothing on this."

Let us study this unique region more closely. The name
Jordan means "the Descender" or "the Down-comer," be-
cause of the rushing descent of the river. *The Jordan* has See opp. p. 36
three (some say four) sources, small streams far up north in
the Hermon Range that unite to form the Upper Jordan.
The longest of these streams, forty miles long, rises 1,700
feet above the sea level, in the *Fountain of Hasbany,* at the
base of a cliff near the village of *Hasbeiya* on the western side
of Mount Hermon. The largest branch is the *Leddan,* rising
at the site of the ancient city of *Dan,* in a clear, deep pool,
the largest single fountain in the world, and from it an im-
mense body of water rushes down the valley, though the

33

elevation of the fountain is not more than 500 feet above the
Sea. Dan was the old *Laish,* and was conquered by the
Danites. (Judges 18.) After the Conquest, the Danites set
up a heretical worship and a graven image for idol service.
(Judg. 18 : 29-31.) Later, at Dan, the worship of the golden
calf was instituted, and it ever thereafter remained a heathen
temple. (1 Kings 12 : 28, 29; Amos 8 : 14.) The third,
and most beautiful, source of the Jordan is at the *Fountain
of Banias,* a stream issuing here, midway in size between
the Leddan and the Hasbany. This source is on the southern base of Mount Hermon. Banias is the equivalent of the
Greek name *Paneas,* the shrine of the god Pan, sacred to the
worship of Baal, the weird god of the Phoenicians, long before the Greeks adapted the grotto to the Pan-god worship,
the shepherd-god. When Rome followed Greece as Master,
Herod the Great built here a temple of exquisite white marble,
in honor of his patron the Emperor Augustus Cæsar. Philip
the Tetrarch, Herod's son, beautified the city and called it
Cæsarea, distinguishing it from the other Cæsarea on the
See opp. p. 36 coast, as *Cæsarea Philippi.* In time, the name Paneas was
restored to it, and the Arabs call it Banias. It marked the
northern limit of our Lord's travels and ministry. Near by
is *Mt. Hermon,* probably the Mount of the Transfiguration.
(S. Matt. 16 : 13-20; 17 : 1-8.) The main source recognized
by the Jews is the one at Banias. From the highest source,
at Hasbeiya down through the Dead Sea, the river is divided
into three sections, three stages or levels, each of which contains a noted lake or sea. The river passes through two of
these lakes and discharges all of its waters into the third.
The most northern and smallest lake in the first basin is
Lake Huleh, known as the *Waters of Merom* in the days of
Joshua, a triangular sheet of water three miles across, situated in an enormous swamp of dense and huge canes and
papyrus, about level with the Mediterranean Sea, never more
than 7 feet above. The second and next largest, the *Lake
of Galilee* called *Lake Chinnereth* in the Old Testament, and
the *Lake of Tiberias* in Christ's time, is a pear-shaped lake,
14 miles long by 9 miles wide, 682 feet below the sea level,
in the section we have studied as Galilee or the Esdraelon

See opp. p. 36

region. The third basin, far south, *the Dead Sea,* the largest
of all, is 46 miles long, with its *surface* 1,290 feet *below* the
Mediterranean, and in some places 1,300 feet deeper still.
Note carefully again, the downward flow of this remarkable
river. At the Hasbeiya Springs, it rises 1,700 feet above the
Sea, Mts. Hermon and Lebanon on either side. At Lake
Merom it is on a level with the Sea. Below Merom, it de-
scends with a fearful drop of 60 feet to the mile, until at
the Sea of Galilee it is 682 feet below the Mediterranean.
Here begins the gorge 65 miles long to the Dead Sea. It
flows so rapidly through the Sea of Galilee that it scarcely
mingles the waters. Along the gorge below it drops 610
feet farther in depth. It flows through the *Plain of Jericho*
on the way, which at this point is a valley 14 miles wide and
400 feet above the level of the Dead Sea, the mountains
around rising to the height of over 3,000 feet. The distance
from Hasbeiya to Lake Merom is about 40 miles, from the
entrance of Merom to the Sea of Galilee about 15 miles,
from the northern end of that Lake to the Dead Sea 79 miles,
making a direct descent in length of 134 miles. During this
descent, it falls over 3,000 feet, an average fall of 22 feet
to the mile. It varies from 80 to 180 feet in width and from
5 to 12 feet in depth.

We will now explore each of these three great basins.
Lake Huleh or *Merom* occupies the lower portion of the
Huleh basin, 12 miles below the site of Dan. At the upper
end of the basin is the huge marsh, of which we spoke, an
area practically impassable, through its reeds and papyrus,
even for a canoe. West of the lake is a rich farming region,
extending to the foot of the mountains. On this plain, by
the *Waters of Merom,* Joshua fought his victorious battle
with the Confederate Kings of the North. (Josh. 11 : 5-8.)
Yet, owing to its malaria and its insecurity from attack, it is
a forsaken, desolate, uninhabited area, not a single permanent
dwelling being found save at the border town of Banias.
From Lake Huleh, it is 11 miles in a straight line to the Lake
of Tiberias. About two miles below the upper lake the
river is spanned by a very ancient bridge, with a ruined khan
at one end, a ford of the Jordan for centuries, and probably

the identical spot that Saul the persecutor crossed on his way from Galilee to Damascus, to imprison the Lord's disciples. The Jordan on leaving Huleh Lake is 60 feet wide and 15 deep, flowing rapidly through a narrow gorge. *The Sea of Galilee* is also called the lake of Tiberias (S. John 6 : 1), the Sea of Chinnereth (Josh. 12 : 3), and the Lake of Gennesaret. (S. Luke 5 : 1.) Its length and breadth we have given. Its depth of water is about 200 feet. On its eastern side, the banks rise 1,000 feet or more. On the west, the Galilean hills descend in terraces, ending in moderate cliffs, with generally a broad belt of lowland between the cliff and the water. On the north, this gradual slope forms the fertile *Plain of Gennesaret*. The entire region is volcanic, and lava and pumice stone lie scattered about everywhere. There are but few trees, and a deserted aspect belongs to it. This Lake is little mentioned in the Old Testament; but is full of incidents of Christ's Life in the New Testament record. In the days of the Romans Gennesaret was a garden spot, all the tiny streams flowing through its plain being utilized, and for ten months each year its orchards and vineyards and fields yielded luxuriant harvests. In our Saviour's day, numerous towns and villages were nestled on its hillsides and lowlands on the western side, and every foot of land was cultivated. On the eastern side, neglect and barreness prevailed, the desert places, to which our Lord so often retired for rest. (See S. Mark 4 : 35, 36; 5 : 21; S. Matt. 14 : 13-15.)

Only two of the many towns of this wonderful Lake, as mentioned by the Evangelists, are now inhabited, *Tiberias* and *Magdala;* and both of these are sadly changed since the See opp. p. 37 glorious days of Rome. We will commence with *Tiberias*, on the western shore about half-way towards the southern end. The city was built by Herod Antipas, and named by him for Tiberius the Emperor. Recent research shows that the enclosing wall was almost three miles long. Huge and splendid buildings were within, a citadel, theaters, amphitheaters, forum, temples, synagogues, baths, dwellings, a noble scene from across the Lake. There is no direct mention of Christ's work there; though he most certainly must have visited it. Near by were noted hot springs, which rendered

KADESH BARNEA

JORDAN RIVER

CAESAREA PHILIPPI
Photo by Williams, Brown & Earle

DEAD SEA

TIBERIAS

MAGDALA
Photo by W. H. Rau

BETHSAIDA OF GALILEE
Photo by S. U. Mitman

BROOK JABBOK
Copyrighted by Underwood & Underwood

the place particularly attractive to the Romans. Its present population is about 5,000. *Magdala* comes next, as we go up the west shore of the Lake. It is the modern village of *Mejdel* (*Migdol* or watch-tower) at the lower end of the See opp. p. 37 Plain of Gennesaret. It was the home of S. Mary of Magdala, the devoted friend of the Master, known in briefer form to-day as the Magdalene. (S. John 20 : 16-18.) The town is also mentioned in S. Matthew 15 : 39, which look up. *Capernaum*, next north, is uncertain as to site (see cut 13); but the most likely one is at the northern end of the Plain. The city undoubtedly stood on a great thoroughfare, roads from it leading in all directions. Of the two sites, one about five miles from the mouth of the Jordan and the other about two, most arguments from the records seem to favor the former. Capernaum was an important Biblical city. It was the home of Jesus after his rejection at Nazareth; it was in fact called "his own city." (S. Matt. 9 : 1.)

Many of our Lord's miracles occurred here, as the healing of the nobleman's son, healing of the demoniac, healing of S. Peter's mother-in-law, first draught of fishes, healing of the paralytic, healing of the Centurion's servant, healing of the blind and dumb demoniacs, raising of Jairus' daughter, healing of a woman with an issue of blood, of the dumb demoniac, and of two blind men, the tribute money in the fish, etc. Here also He called Levi or Matthew the Publican. Two at least of His Apostles, S. Peter and S. Matthew, had homes here, and after the rejection at Nazareth His mother, S. Mary, transferred her own home here. (See S. Mark 1 : 29; 2 : 14, 15; S. Matt. 12 : 46; S. John 2 : 12. Also S. Matt. 8 : 14-17; S. Mark 1 : 21-34; S. Luke 4 : 33-41.) The town of *Bethsaida of Galilee* is just above Capernaum. Note also the other *Bethsaida Julias*, which lies a little east and See opp. p. 37 north, up the Jordan. The former Bethsaida certainly lay near Capernaum (S. Mark 6 : 45; S. John 6 : 17), with a jutting headland between them. Some ruined buildings and an octagonal fountain mark the probable site. This town was the birthplace of S. Peter, S. Andrew, and S. Philip. Above this Bethsaida may have been *Chorazin,* but its site is really unknown. (See S. Matt. 11 : 21.) *Bethsaida Julias* was

originally a small fishing town.   Later it was enlarged by
Philip the Tetrarch and given to his daughter, Julias, hence
its name. On a slope near by, our Lord fed the Five Thousand. (S. Luke 9 : 10-17.)   On a mountain adjacent He was
praying alone when the storm broke over the disciples, on
their way across the Lake to Bethsaida of Galilee. (S. Mark
6 : 45, 46; S. John 6 : 15-17.)   *Gergesa* may have been where
the ruins of a town called *Gersa, or Khersa* on the eastern
shore of the Lake, have recently been discovered. It may
have given its name to the surrounding country. (S. Matt.
8 : 28.)   The healing of the demoniacs occurred here and
the destruction of the herd of swine. (S. Luke 8 : 26; S.
Matt. 8 : 28-34.)   The modern railroad to Damascus runs
up the Lake to Gersa, and thence turns eastward.

The Lake of Galilee is noted to-day for its sudden and
violent storms. On it was the stilling of the tempest. On it
S. Peter walked to Jesus. It was renowned the world over for
its variety and unusual abundance of fish, and the two
miraculous draughts of fishes came from its bosom. To-day,
not more than fifteen or sixteen small boats ply the entire
Lake, and they may often be seen all together, tied up at
Capernaum.

Questions and Manual Work on Chapter VII.

1. Write down fifteen chief localities and events of the
Third Zone of Palestine, the great mountainous backbone or
ridge.

2. Tell all you can, in description, of Jerusalem and its
environs.

3. Make a new outline map of Palestine, and draw in the
full Jordan Valley and River System.

4. Take an outline map of Esdraelon and Sea of Galilee
(Bailey or Bible Study Co., S. S. Commission) and place each
city and special locality (mountain, etc.), in the Galilee region,
studied thus far.

5. Make a list of these cities and the events and Bible
references.

CHAPTER VIII

THE REMAINDER OF THE JORDAN VALLEY

The Fourth Zone of Palestine.

The natives call the *Valley of the Jordan,* lying between the Lake and the Dead Sea, *the Ghor,* that is the gorge or rift, 65 miles long. On both sides the highlands rise up from 2,000 to 3,000 feet. The winds sweep across the top of these mountains, making the Ghor itself of the utmost tropical climate, a veritable hotbed. Two rivers flow into the Jordan on its way south, both coming from the east. They are *the Yarmuk* or *Jarmuk* or *Hieromax,* entering four miles from the foot of the Lake; and *the Jabbok* which comes in about See opp. p. 37 twenty miles above the Dead Sea. Within the Ghor lies an inner, smaller, and deeper valley, known as *the Zor.* At the north, it is but 20 feet below in depth; but at the south it is fully 200 feet deeper. Its width varies from one-fourth of a mile to two miles. It is jungle of tropical growth, and filled, even now, with wild animals,—wolves, leopards, and formerly lions being among them. Still again, within the Zor, at a lower level, runs the tortuous, dashing Jordan, from 100 to 200 feet wide usually; but in the rainy season a veritable flood, covering the entire Zor ofttimes. (See Jer. 12 : 5; 49 : 19; 50 : 44; Zech. 11 : 3; Josh. 3 : 15; 1 Chron. 12 : 15.)

The *Fords of the Jordan* are numerous. The river is from three to ten feet deep, and in ancient times there was not a bridge the whole way down. The Hebrew language did not possess a word for bridge. There were few towns along this Jordan Valley, partly on account of the river and partly from the prevailing malaria, the danger of invasion from wild beasts and hostile robber tribes from the eastern side of the river. On the western side, we have

Beth-shan, at the foot of the *Valley of Jezreel,* on the brow of the hill as it drops. It was held by Canaanites, though allotted to Manasseh. (Judg. 1 : 27.) Ten miles south of Beth-shan was *Abel Meholah,* the Meadow of the Dance, whence the Midianites fled (Judg. 7 : 22) and where Elisha lived, before he became a prophet. (1 Kings 19 : 15-18.)

The *city of Adam* was probably near the mouth of the Jabbok, on the east side of the Valley. (See especially, Josh. 3 : 16.) *Zaretan,* which has not been placed, was near this same river, and the district of Zaretan we know extended all along that region. *Succoth,* the place of booths, has been fixed as about a mile north of the *Damieh Ford,* which lies just below the junction of the Jabbok and the Jordan. Here Jacob dwelt for a time and built booths for his cattle. (Gen. 33 : 16, 17.) Solomon's brass foundries were also near this See opp. p. 52 place. (1 Kings 7 : 46.) *Jericho,* a very important city, was situated on the western side of the Valley, here a great broad plain, about six miles from the Jordan, a mile and a half above the modern town of that name. It was the first city captured by the Israelites in the actual conquest of the land, after the wanderings in the wilderness following the Exodus. (Read Joshua 2.) Its beautiful groves of palms gave it the name *City of Palm Trees.* (Deut. 34 : 3.) It was a very wealthy city at the Conquest. (Josh. 6 : 19; 7 : 2.) The city walls then fell under providential interposition, though God, here, as elsewhere, may have used natural means, for since walls were not built strongly in those ancient days, it may well have been that the steady rhythmic stamp of many marching feet may have set up vibrations that rendered the wall quite ready to topple over when the mighty shout went up. In Christ's time the new Jericho, built below, was a noted and famous city, beautified by Herod the Great with wonderful palaces and architectural splendors. Here too the great king died. In the old Jericho, Rahab lived. (Josh. 2; 6 : 22-25.) On its fall, the curse was proclaimed against any one ever rebuilding its walls. (Josh. 6 : 26.) In the time of Ahab, Hiel of Bethel tried to revive it, and fell under the curse. (1 Kings 16 : 30-34.) One of the Schools of the Prophets was situated at

(2 See opp. p. 52

Jericho, a school which both Elijah and Elisha visited. (2
Kings 2.) It should be carefully noted that there have really
been three Jerichos. We have mentioned the original one and
also the Roman one, farther south. The modern one, probably not older than the twelfth century, was in between the
two, as we have said not two miles from the original city.
It is a small Arab village of rough houses. Very recently a
hotel and a Russian Hospice have been erected there. *Gilgal,* the first camping spot of the Israelites after crossing
Jordan, lay a little south and east of the ancient Jericho on
the Plain. Here the twelve stones of the river bed were
set up for a memorial, after the passage of the stream. (Josh.
4 : 19.) Here the rite of circumcision was renewed. (Josh.
5 : 2.)

At Gilgal, the Passover was celebrated and the manna
ceased when the march reached this city. (Josh. 5 : 12.)
Gilgal was also the resting-place of the ark until it was re-
moved to Shiloh. Somewhere on the Plain on its western
side, probably in the south, near the northern end of the
Sea, stood the *Cities of the Plain, Sodom, Gomorrah, Admah,
Zoar, and Zeboim,* which were overwhelmed with destruction
in the time of Abraham. It may even be the site once held
by these fated cities that is now beneath a portion of the
Dead Sea, for the Sea undoubtedly occupied a larger area
in ancient times. The Bible descriptions of their destruction
(Gen. 19; Deut. 29 : 23; Isa. 1 : 9; 3 : 9; 13 : 19; Jer. 23 :
14; 49 : 18; 50 : 40; Lam. 4 : 6; Ezek. 16 : 46, 53; Amos
4 : 11) seem to indicate a bitumen or petroleum or pitch
eruption, similar to such as have occurred in the oil regions
of America, due to compressed gases, intermingled with oil
and water, forming flaming fire coming down from above,
with cinders, smoke, ejected water, which last would supply
the encrustations that may have formed the pillar of salt out
of Lot's ill-fated wife. It is a remarkable proof of the influence of climate, country, and environment, that, as Professor Kent has pointed out, every race and tribe that came in
and settled on this low, miasmic, tropical Plain of the Jordan Valley became in time corrupt and degenerate, morally,
physically, and even mentally; whereas those in the moun-

tainous regions, whether native or moving up from the Valley, were hardy, sturdy, high-minded, intellectual, moral for the most part, and a better race of men. Environment does mold character to a most important degree. Nearly opposite Jericho, across the Jordan, on the eastern side of the Valley, lay *the Plains of Moab, the Plain of Abel Shittim,* the meadow of the Acacias, extending from this point nearly down to the head of the Dead Sea, about fifteen miles by eight. It is still dotted with ancient, gnarled acacias, descendants of the Shittah trees of the days of Moses. (Num. 22 : 1; Josh. 3 : 1; Num. 33 : 49.) In later days, although assigned to Reuben and Gad, and specked with their fortified cities, the only remains of which to-day are heaps of earth or tells, it fell under the Amorites and became their land. Of the several Fords of the Jordan, the one of importance is *Damieh Ford,* just below the junction of the Jabbok, the crossing-place from Mount Gilead to Shechem, where Jacob crossed on his return from Padan Aram, and where the Ephraimites who could not pronounce "Shibboleth" were discovered and killed. (Gen. 12 : 6; 33 : 18; Judg. 12 : 5, 6.) *The Nimrim Ford* is opposite Jericho, often known as *the Upper Ford,* the main thoroughfare to the opposite shore. Over this ford the ark was borne at the Conquest (Josh. 3, 15, 16); here Elijah and Elisha parted the waters; and here, probably, our Lord was baptized. (S. John 1 : 28.) *The Lower Ford,* known as the *Pilgrims' Bathing Place,* is five miles below, and was used as the fords towards Moab. Ehud, Ruth and Naomi all crossed it. (Judg. 3 : 28; Ruth 1.)

The Dead Sea, of which we have spoken, is mentioned in the Bible as *the Salt Sea,* the *Sea of the Plain,* the *Sea of Arabah.* (See Josh. 3 : 16; Deut. 4 : 49; 2 Kings 14 : 25.) Its shore is desolate, lined with rock-salt and cakes of pitch, save the southeastern corner, which is fertile through fresh springs. Here at this eastern side too is the distinguishing promontory or peninsula of *El Lisan* (the tongue), 12 miles long and 6 wide. The Sea is more than five times as salty as the ocean, and extremely bitter to taste.

Questions and Manual Work on Chapter VIII.

1. Make a sand table map of Palestine, in fullest detail, at least 3 x 4 feet. Let it be carefully worked out, spending the whole hour (or more) on it. Mark cities by lentils (Haimel's); the mountains by pole men (S. S. Commission sets), etc. Put pin-flags for battlefields.

2. Let the class members quiz each other on the events located at the various cities, battlefields, etc.

3. Locate in detail and discuss the cities of the Jordan Valley below the Sea of Galilee.

CHAPTER IX

THE FIFTH ZONE OF PALESTINE.   THE EASTERN
TABLE LAND

Climbing up the hills of Moab and Gilead, we are in **the Fifth Zone of Palestine,** in the midst of rolling, grass-covered hills, cut by rifting ravines, with dashing mountain torrents. This zone is almost entirely a highland country, its general elevation being 2,000 feet above the Sea. The backbone of the mountains is the *Anti-Lebanon range,* lower and more irregular than the Lebanon range. It is mostly a series of broken, parallel ridges. Beginning far in the north, a little above Damascus, we see a marked depression or break, separating the East Mountain of the Anti-Lebanon Range from Mount Hermon. This depression has formed the natural caravan route from Beirut to Damascus. The southern end of this upper range is broken by the deep valley of the See opp. p. 52 *river Abana, the Barada* of modern times. (2 Kings 5 : 12.) In a bend in the Abana river is the old site of *Abila,* the capital of Abilene, mentioned by S. Luke, in connection with See opp. p. 52 the Tetrarchy of Lysanias. (S. Luke 3 : 1.) *Damascus* is situated on a fertile plain, at the foot of Mount Hermon. It is watered by the beautiful Abana, which divides into many small streams, watering thus the Plain. Its surplus waters gather and are lost in a Lake at the edge of the Plain, on the borders of the desert. Probably no city of present-day existence can trace its history so far back as can Damascus. In the Bible it is often called Syria. Routes of travel lay through it in all directions. Hundreds of canals and rivulets murmur through the City and the Plain, making 150 square miles of delightful green, in the midst of which is the white, compact City and picturesque minarets. *The Awaj River,* supposed to be *the Pharpar,* rises on the sides of

44

Mount Hermon and flows across the Plain, a few miles below the Abana, entering another lake, below the twin marsh lakes of the Abana. (See 2 Kings 5 : 12.) The present population of Damascus is not less than 250,000. Abram visited Damascus, and his chief servant, Eliezer, came from that town. (Gen. 15 : 2.) Its first mention in the Bible is in connection with the pursuit of Chedorlaomer. (Gen. 14 : 15.) David set a garrison there (2 Sam. 8 : 6) and it became part of Solomon's Kingdom. (1 Chron. 18 : 6.) Hazael came from Damascus. (2 Kings 8.) It became the capital of Syria in the days of that pushing Kingdom. Hither Saul was journeying, to seize and imprison Christians, when he was vouchsafed a vision from God and Jesus Christ was manifested to him. Here he was baptized and restored to normal sight. (Acts 9 : 1-26.) He revisited the City later and preached boldly in the name of Christ. (Gal. 1 : 17.) From See opp. p. 53 that city he escaped in a basket. (Acts 9 : 24, 25.) Look up the many references to Damascus, noting its power and prestige, and its important place in the history of the Israelites. (2 Sam. 8 : 3; 10 : 6; 1 Kings 4 : 21; 11 : 23; 15 : 18, 19; 20 : 1-34; 22 : 1-40; 2 Kings 6 : 24; 7; 8 : 28; 10 : 32; 12 : 17; 13 : 25; 14 : 28; 15 : 37; 16 : 5.) Its final overthrow is noted in Amos 1 : 5.

EASTERN PALESTINE, as we journey southward, has three main divisions, Bashan, Gilead, and Moab. BASHAN extends from the base of Mount Hermon and the Pharpar river to the Jarmuk or Hieromax river. This division is again divided into sections. The northern section is *the district of Jedur,* the *Iturea* of S. Luke. (S. Luke 3 : 1.) It extended probably to the northern end of Lake Huleh. The Hagarites or Ishmaelites dwelt there. The name Jedur was derived from Jetur, a son of Ishmael. (Gen. 25 : 15.) The divisions of Bashan south of the Jedur are longitudinal. Next to the Jordan side, from Jedur's lower limit to the Jarmuk, was *the Jaulan,* named so from Golan, its chief city, a City of Refuge under Moses. (Deut. 4 : 43; Josh. 20 : 8; 21 : 27.) *The Kingdom of Geshur* was in this district. One of David's wives was a daughter of the king of Geshur, and her son, Absalom, fled to this region. (Deut. 3 : 14; Josh.

13 : 13; 2 Sam. 15 : 8; 1 Chron. 2 : 23.) Roman Gaulanitis must have been about equal to the same region. *The Hauran district* comes next, a level, treeless plain 50 miles long and 15 or 20 miles wide, of loose, volcanic soil, very fertile and well-tilled. The Hauran Plain is bordered on the east, between it and the desert, by *the Lejah or "Refuge"* of the Arabs, the rough region called therefore *Trachonitis* by the Greeks. (S. Luke 3 : 1.) It was also known as *Argob,* the "stony," by the Hebrews. (Deut. 3 : 4.) It is a vast mass of congealed lava, 350 square miles, or 60 miles in circumference, a black, motionless sea, with waves of petrified lava, dotted with the remains of ancient towns, for it was the stronghold of *the Kingdom of Og.* (See especially Deut. 3 : 4, 5; 3 : 14; 1 Kings 4 : 13. Recall also the reference in Psalms. Psa. 135 : 11; 136 : 20.) *Edrei* on the southern border of the Lejah was the capital, and the battlefield where Og lost his life. (Deut. 3 : 1; Num. 21 : 33; Josh. 12 : 4; 13 : 12.) *Kenath or Nobah* was also in the southeastern extremity. (Look up Num. 22 : 42; 1 Chron. 2 : 23; Num. 32 : 42; Judg. 8 : 4-11.) Some sixty other cities, "the giant cities of Bashan," were scattered over this Plain. Their ruins are still there, intermingled with magnificent remains of Greek and Roman architecture, and inscriptions dedicated to the many Christian martyrs of Decian and Diocletian Persecutions. *Job's country, the Land of Uz,* was in Southern Bashan, if we may trust traditions of the Arabs. The weight of present-day authority places Uz on the border of the desert near Petra, in the land of Edom. The extent of Bashan is about 130 miles, north and south, and from Jordan Valley to the desert. THE LAND OF GILEAD extends sixty miles from the Jarmuk to the head of the Dead Sea, at the Heshbon river. (Josh. 22 : 9.) *The Jarmuk or Hieromax* is nearly the size of the Jordan, where it enters that river. *The Brook Jabbok* cuts across a little below half way down Gilead. The part above is Northern Gilead, that below is Southern, and belonged at the Conquest to Sihon, King of the Amorites. (Num. 21 : 24-26; Josh. 13 : 25; Judg. 11 : 21, 22; Psa. 136 : 19.) Gilead is more elevated than Bashan; there is less of volcanic deposit and more of limestone; many forests of

noble trees, among them the *Wood of Ephraim,* that spelled
the Waterloo of Absalom. (2 Sam. 18 : 6-14.) "The Balm
of Gilead" has been sought for among these forest trees but
thus far has not been discovered. Gilead was the country
of Jepthah, the Judge of Manasseh, and of Elijah. The
southern portion was *the Kingdom of the Ammonites.* That
portion, together with the upper part of Moab, i.e. from the
Jabbok to the Arnon, was *the Perea* of the New Testament,
where one part of our Lord's Ministry was fulfilled and
along the border of which he was baptized. (See S. Matt.
19 : 1, 13; S. Mark 10 : 1; S. Luke 13 : 22; S. John 10 : 40.)
Mount Pisgah, (*Jebel Osha*) is the highest mountain peak, the
most sightly place in all Palestine, save Mount Hermon. It
is an isolated peak on the southern side of the Jabbok, "over
against Jericho." From this point of vantage Moses viewed
the Promised Land. (Deut. 34 : 1.) From these heights
Balaam viewed the Camp of the Israelites. (Num. 24 : 5-9.)
Some of the important cities of Gilead are now studied.
Gadara is *the Um-Keis* of to-day, three miles south of the
Jarmuk, and five miles east of Jordan. It was in the country of the Gadarenes, the site of the healing of the demoniacs.
(S. Matt. 8 : 28; S. Mark 5 : 1; S. Luke 8 : 26.) The ruins
of *Gadara* are over two miles in circumference. The site
of *Mahanaim* is unsettled. All Bible references seem to indicate it as located north of the Jabbok in the land assigned
to Gad, near the border of Manasseh. (Gen. 32 : 2; Josh.
13 : 30; 21 : 38.) At this spot, Jacob met the angels of
God. Here Ishbosheth was crowned and later slain. Here
David fled from the pursuit of Absalom. Here, in the gate,
he waited for the news of the battle fought, and in the
chamber over the gate he wept sore for his rebellious son.
(See 2 Sam. 2 : 8; 4 : 5; 17 : 24; 18 : 24-33.)

Jabesh-Gilead is identified as probably straight across
country from Dothan, at the modern Ed-Deir. It is important for connection with the following events : the defec-
tion of Benjamin (Judg. 21 : 8-14) ; the route of the hosts of
Ammon (1 Sam. 11 : 1-11) ; and the rescue of the bodies of
Saul and Jonathan. (1 Sam. 31 : 11, 12; 2 Sam. 2 : 5.) *Pella*
is six miles northwest of Jabesh-Gilead. It is the city to

which the Christians of Jerusalem fled just before the siege of Titus. *Peniel or Penuel* was on the Brook Jabbok; but exactly where is uncertain. Here Jacob wrestled with the angel. (Gen. 32.) *Gerasa* was a city of note, about twenty miles east of the Jordan, on one of the northern branches of the Jabbok. It was also called Jerash. It is considered the most perfect Roman city existing above ground to-day, for more than 200 magnificent buildings are still standing. It was one of the chief members of the Decapolis, ten cities that, at the opening of the Christian period, banded together in a confederacy of Greek-speaking people for mutual defense and trade propaganda. These cities were all on the great highroads of Eastern Palestine, only Beth-shean, the ancient Scythopolis, being to the west. Each city had an outlying country district. Later more than ten cities were included. The cultured and wealthy of that part of the world were gathered in them. Christ visited many of them in this region. Once so throbbing with life, this section to-day is deserted, and even the sites of most of its towns are gone. Heaps of desolate ruins are all that mark ancient sites of a wondrous civilization. *Ramoth-Gilead* is another of the disputed sites, the city where Ahab died (1 Kings 22 : 34) ; the city which Hazael captured (2 Kings 8 : 28; 9 : 14) ; the city where Jehu was proclaimed king (2 Kings 9 : 4. See also Deut. 4 : 43; 1 Kings 4 : 13.) It was also a City of Refuge. That is was somewhere in this general locality seems, however, certain. *Mizpah* is supposed to be *Suf,* a village three miles south of Geresa, where Jacob and Laban erected "a heap of witnesses," a monument of stone to seal their covenant. (Gen. 31 : 44.) *Rabbath-Ammon*, the ancient capital of the Ammonites, is on the south side of the Arnon, to the east. Israel did not purpose to make war on either Ammon or Moab, since they were descendants of Lot. But they hired Balaam to come to curse Israel, and Joab in the time of David captured Rabbath. In front of its walls, Uriah the Hittite was slain. (See Deut. 2 : 9, 19; Num. 22; 2 Sam. 11 : 1; 12 : 26.) In New Testament times, this was called *Philadelphia.* The ruins of Philadelphia are still extant. *The Land of Moab* lies to the east of the Dead Sea, from the Arnon down about fifteen miles. It is a treeless plateau, 4,300 feet above the Dead Sea. It was held by the Moabites, though they also claimed some land north of the Arnon, during certain periods.

In this land Elimelech and Naomi found refuge and David trusted his aged parents to the king of Moab, although later he waged a bitter war against these people. (See Judg. 11 : 12-18; Ruth 1; 4 : 9; S. Matt. 1 : 5-15; 1 Sam. 22 : 3; 2 Sam. 8 : 2.) Among the cities of Biblical interest we mention *Beth-peor* just east of the head of the Salt Sea, the burial-place of Moses. (Josh. 13 : 20; Deut. 34 : 6.) *Heshbon* lies farther east on the same straight line, on a lofty elevation, 200 feet above the surrounding Plain, fifteen miles east of the Sea. Heshbon was the capital of the Amorite king, Sihon, who captured it from the Moabites. (Num. 21 : 26.) Later it was captured by the Moabites again. (Isa. 15 : 4; Jer. 48 : 34; Josh. 21 : 39.) Six miles south of Heshbon is *Medeba,* before which Joab fought a terrific battle with the combined forces of Syria and Ammon, winning the day for Israel. (1 Chron. 19 : 6.) *Dibon* is on a straight line, 9 or 10 miles south of Medeba. It is mentioned in Num. 21 : 30; 33 : 34; Isa. 15 : 2. Here it was that Dr. Klein discovered the famous Moabite Stone in 1868, a black basalt slab 3½ by 2 feet in size, now in the Louvre at Paris. It records an important account of the oppression of Moab by Omri of Israel and the deliverance under Mesha of Moab. It is dated 900 B. C. The characters are in Phoenician. (See 2 Kings 3 : 3-5.) *Kir of Moab* lies about six miles south of the Arnon. It was a noted Moabite stronghold. (Num. 21 : 28; Isa. 15 : 1; 2 Kings 3 : 26.) Here Mesha was besieged by the forces of Israel and Edom.

Edom or Mt. Seir, called *Idumea* in the New Testament, is the strip of hilly country just south of Moab, lying between the Desert of Arabia and the Wilderness of Paran. *The Brook Zered* separates it from Moab on the north. This Zered was the stream which Israel crossed, under the orders that terminated their long period of wanderings in the wilderness, and began their onward march of conquest into the Promised Land. (See Num. 21 : 12 and Deut. 2 : 13, 14.)

Ancient Edom was 100 miles long and about 20 wide. *Mount Hor* is along its eastern border towards the north. On the top to-day is a Muhammadan temple, erected over the traditional site of Aaron's tomb. (Num. 20 : 23; 33 : 37.) *Bozrah,* the old capital of Edom, lies at the northern portion. *Petra or Selah* is near Mt. Hor. (2 Kings 14 : 7.) It possesses a marvelous rock-hewn Roman temple. When Chedorlaomer swept over Mount Seir or Edom, the country was occupied by the Horites, or mountaineers. (Gen. 14 : 6.) During the Exodus, the Edomites forbade the Israelites passage through their land. (Num. 20 : 14.) They were conquered by David and held subject to his successors. (2 Sam. 8 : 14; 2 Kings 8 : 20; 14 : 1-8; 2 Chron. 25 : 1-14; 28 : 17.) They united with Chaldea against Judah, and were condemned for this action. (Psa. 137 : 7; Ezek. 25 : 12.) Later they were overthrown by the Amalekites from south of the Negeb. The Nabatheans, descendants of Ishmael, then overran the country. Aretas, their king, was father-in-law to Herod Antipas.

Questions and Manual Work on Chapter IX.

1. Take a sheet of paper 8 x 12 inches. Fold three times the short way and four times the long way. Get a Hebrew World Map of Bailey Series and rule it off the same way as the paper is creased. Transfer by the eye the enlargement to your folded sheet. The Coast Line of the Great Sea falls within the upper squares of the second row. The point of Sinai peninsula falls in the same vertical line. The Euphrates and Tigris rivers lie across the upper and middle third tiers and the middle right tier. Palestine Proper lies entirely within the middle second tier.

2. Locate on this map, which we will call the Eastern Bible World, the places noted in this Chapter.

3. Make a list of the places, their names, events of historical interest, and Bible references.

CHAPTER X

The Plain of Esdraelon

One zone of Palestine yet remains to be explored, the Sixth, as Professor Kent terms it, far up north. It is the PLAIN OF ESDRAELON, and, unlike all the others, it cuts across the Central Plateau from east to west. It is a rough triangle, one angle being at Mount Carmel, one down south in the hills of Samaria, and the third at Mount Tabor and Galilee. It is a huge, level, treeless plain, watered by the muddy Kishon. It has been called the key to Palestine, for its valleys connect in every direction with all the other zones. It has, through all ages, been the great battlefield of the nations. Esdraelon is the Greek word for *Jezreel,* which is translated "God's sowing," a tribute to the extreme fertility of this plain. The main section of the plain is often called the *Valley of Megiddo.* Among the noted battles, the fields of which were almost clearly visible to our blessed Lord when as a youth or man he climbed the hills within a few minutes' walk from his home at Nazareth, scenes that must have stirred his patriotic heart to a tumult are the following:—Deborah's battle with the Canaanites occurred at Mount Tabor when Sisera was slain by the wife of Heber the Kenite (Judg. 5, 6); and Gideon's victory over the Midianites at Mount Gilboa, with the hosts of Midian at *Mt. Moreh.* Here is still Gideon's Spring, where the 300 lapped water, and put to flight Midian and Amalek. (Judg. 6. 7.) On this great battlefield, near Shunem, Saul and Jonathan were slain by the Philistines, who had come up the Maritime Plain and into Esdraelon by way of Megiddo. (1 Sam. 28.) Still again, the saddest defeat Israel ever met, and the one that decided forever her overthrow, was the

death of the promising young king Josiah on the Plain of
Megiddo, as Pharaoh-Necho, the monarch of Egypt, sought
to battle with the king of Babylon. Josiah had been Israel's
hope, a good king and a reformer, and with his death all
her hopes vanished. (2 Kings 23 : 28; 2 Chron. 35 : 20.)
Here Jehu met his doom, as he raged in his chariot up the
Valley of Jezreel, striving against the kings of Israel and
Judah. (2 Kings 9.) The Maccabees, the Romans, the
Arabs, the Crusaders, and Napoleon himself all fought and
struggled on this same sacred ground. The author of Revelation called it Armageddon, in token of its many conflicts.
(Rev. 16 : 16.)

Let us locate some of these most historic places. *Megiddo,*
now known as *Lejjun,* lies about the center of the lower
border of the Plain, in the general direction of the continua-
tion, southeasterly, of the Carmel range of mountains. *Taanach,* mentioned five times in the Bible in connection with
Megiddo, was a stronghold of the Canaanites, situated four
or five miles southeast of Megiddo. Not far from it is
Hadad Rimmon, where the great mourning for Josiah was
held. (Zech. 12 : 11.) Half-way over to the Valley of the
Jordan and a little to the north lies *Jezreel,* the modern
Zerin, now a collection of rude huts, formerly the magnificent
royal residence of Ahab and his evil court. Gideon and
Saul, Elijah and Naboth, Joram, Ahaziah, and Jehu, all had
to do with this city. (1 Kings 21 ; 2 Kings 9 : 34.) Traveling northeast, we come to *Shunem,* the home of the Shu-
nammite woman whose guest-room was open to Elisha, and
whose son the prophet restored to life. (2 Kings 4.) Abishag
dwelt there, and also the fair woman of Canticles. (1 Kings
1 : 3, 4; Cant. 6 : 13.)

The Valley of Jezreel is the eastern extension of the Plain
of Esdraelon. It is watered chiefly by the *Brook Jalud,*
emptying into the Jordan, and rising in the *Ain Jalud, the
Fountain of Jezreel,* at the foot of Mount Gilboa. This is the
supposed *Fountain or Spring of Gideon.* (Judg. 7.) Here,
too, king Saul camped, just previous to his defeat and death.
(1 Sam. 28 : 4; 29 : 1 ; 31 : 1.) Far over, southeast, towards
the Jordan Valley, is *Bethshan or Scythopolis,* an old strong-

RUINS OF NEW TESTAMENT
JERICHO

FOUNTAIN OF ELISHA
Photo by S. U. Mitman

RIVER ABANA
Photo by S. U. Mitman

DAMASCUS IN THE
DISTANT BACKGROUND

DAMASCUS,
Street called Straight

BALBEC RUINS IN
DISTANCE

ANTIOCH IN SYRIA
Photo by W. H. Rau

ANTIOCH OF PISIDIA
Photo by W. H. Rau

hold of the Canaanites, held by them long after the Conquest. (Judg. 1 : 27.) The bodies of Saul and Jonathan were hung on its walls and rescued from there by the men of Jabesh-Gilead. (1 Sam. 31 : 12-13.) There are three mountains of importance in this Plain of Esdraelon, all of them connected with decisive events. From the north downwards, we see *Mount Tabor,* near the foot of the Sea of Tiberias, the most noticeable landmark in lower Galilee. It is not a ridge, but a single mountain, a cone, cut off at the top. From Mount Tabor, the view reaches to the Mediterranean, to Mount Ebal, and to Mount Hermon. Here Barak and Deborah met; here the brothers of Gideon were slain; here some traditions place the Transfiguration of our Lord, though it is unlikely that it occurred at this spot. (Judg. 4 : 5; 8 : 18.) *Little Hermon, or the Hill of Moreh,* is the next mountain, across the valley southward, historic by reason of Gideon's victory (Judg. 7 : 1) and of Saul's witch of Endor. (1 Sam. 28 : 4, 7-25.) The village of *Nain* is on the side of the mountain towards the north, where was restored to life the son of the widow of Nain. (S. Luke 7 : 11.) *Endor* is but two miles northeast of Nain on the same slope of the mountain. In addition to its connection with the witch episode, it was the spot where Barak slew the chiefs of the Canaanites. (Psa. 83 : 10.) The third mountain, still farther south, is *Mount Gilboa,* a ridge or range, about ten miles, from 500 to 1,500 feet high in part. *Jezreel* is on a spur at one end, while *Bethshan* is at the other. On the northern slope Saul and Jonathan met their fate. (2 Sam. 1 : 19.)

Questions and Manual Work on Chapter X.

1. Take a Bailey Map of Esdraelon and mark on it in red ink the sites of all cities, places, mountains, valleys, etc., of which you have learned in this or previous lessons. Put flags for the battlefields.

2. How many and what battlefields were there? What crises did they determine?

3. What places were visited by our Lord?

4. In which ones did He perform miracles and what?

5. Make a paper-pulp map of Esdraelon and color in inks.

CHAPTER XI

THE EASTERN EMPIRES

Far over across *the Arabian Desert,* known as the *Land of Uz or Kedar,* we come to another section of Asia, also a Bible land, which we must hastily explore. From the great highlands of present-day **Armenia,** over 7,000 feet above the sea, there stretches a mighty plain, 700 miles to the Persian Gulf, lying between the great rivers, *the Euphrates* on the west and *the Tigris* on the east. It has been called the *Land of the Twin Rivers.* The upper section was named PADAN ARAM, and later, by the Greeks, *Mesopotamia* or the Land between the Rivers. The lower portion was **Shinar or Caldea.** The northern division is mountainous limestone and gypsum. The lower is low-level land, reclaimed from the ocean below by filling-in from the deposits of earth carried down by the rivers. It is still growing at the rate of over 75 feet a year. The lower plain has not a mineral or stone of any kind. Both the rivers rise, one on either side of *Lake Van,* in Armenia, 150 miles apart. The entire country to-day is a scene of barrenness and desolation, inhabited only by wandering Bedouin Arabs. The cities have disappeared, and only tells, or mounds of earth, mark their sites. These tells are the heaps of ruined walls and houses, all having been made of clay bricks, which in the long years have disintegrated and crumbled away. Beneath these mounds are the lost cities. In 1820 men began to seek out these ancient cities and explore them. From the middle of this past century on, great explorers and men of science and learning have devoted lives and money to the labor of digging out the buried ruins, and rich biblical treasures have amply repaid them.

We will begin with **Caldea,** also called *Shinar* and *Babylonia,* in the south. This is the plain south of *Bagdad.* The

54

early inhabitants were Cushites, of the stock of Ham. *Ur of the Caldees (Mugheir)* was the birthplace of Abram. The first empire began there, probably in 2800 B. C., and lasted till about 538 B. C. Babylon then became the capital. *Borsippa* is the ruins of Birs Nimrud, near Babylon, the supposed situation of the Tower of Babel. The remains of the stage tower seem to have been identified. *Nippur, Nifur,* is on the canal or *River Chebar,* in the central part of the plain south of Babylon. It was the sanctuary of the heathen god, Bel. A wonderful library has been brought to light here, some tablets being as ancient as 2000 B. C.

Above Babylon lies **Mesopotamia,** *Aram-naharaim, the Syria* of the Two Rivers. The northern part contains *Orfa* or *Edessa* and *Haran,* Abram's city of sojourn on the way to Canaan. Mesopotamia is mentioned in the Bible only once as a kingdom (Judg. 3 : 8), for later it was a part of the rising kingdom of Assyria.

The next tier of kingdoms, looking eastward, begins with **Armenia** on the north, a translation of the name Ararat, on some mountain peak of which Noah's Ark rested after the flood. (Gen. 8 : 4.) Next south comes **Assyria,** always *Asshur* in the Bible, now the kingdom of Kurdistan, a mountain range separating it from Armenia on the north. It runs half-way down the Tigris on the south. *Nineveh,* the capital of Assyria under Sennacherib (700 B. C.), is on the east bank of the Tigris, towards the north. Very recently it has been unearthed and explored. The wonderful palace of this king is being uncovered, supposed to have been the most extensive and magnificent in the world. Seventy-one rooms have already been explored. Enormous libraries of clay tablet brick books have been uncovered, all written in cuneiform or wedge-shaped letters on baked clay, containing records of untold value both for history and for the corroboration of the Bible. The famous library of Asshurbanipal is among them. The books are being gradually translated and published. The story of the archæological discoveries in Babylonia, Palestine and Egypt reads like tales of entrancing adventure, and will well repay farther study by the reader. **Calah,** the ruins of *Nimrud,* is 18 miles below Nineveh, on the Tigris. It was an early capital. (Gen. 10 : 11.) It was here that the great Black Obelisk was found. *Dur-sharrukin,* where Sargon's palace was built, covering more than 25 acres, is 18 miles northeast of Nineveh. It is probable that all the four cities noted in Genesis 10 : 11, 12 were within the wall surrounding Nineveh. **Elam or Susiana** lies next south, between *the Zagros Mountains* and the Tigris River. *Susa or Shushan* was its capital, and later on the capital of the Medo-Persian empire. The mound that covers it is partly unearthed. The palace of Esther has been discovered. (Esther 1.) The most important "find" is a cut slab with the law code of Khammurabi, king of Shinar in the time of Abram, many of the laws being closely akin to the laws of Moses in the Bible.

On the east of the *Persian Gulf* lies **Persia,** a small land, and mostly a barren region. *Persepolis,* in the center, one of its ancient capitals, has splendid ruins, showing it to have been a great city once. Persia did not rise into power until Babylon fell, 536 B. C. It then ruled over all lands from India to Ethiopia and became the greatest of all the empires. It was overthrown by Alexander the Great in 330 B. C. Its capital then was Susa, Shushan, of which we have learned.

Still farther east, reaching to the Caspian Sea and beyond, lies **Media,** the old *Madai.* (Gen. 10 : 2.) The Medes were of Aryan or Japhetic descent. The empire of Media arose in 633 B. C., conquered Assyria, Armenia, and Persia, and became the Medo-Persian Empire, overcoming the Babylonian in 536 B. C., afterwards to be swallowed up by Persia. It is part of the kingdom of Persia to-day. The Persians who come to America are from the neighborhood of *Lake Urumiah,* to the east of the Caspian Sea.

Syria, the Hebrew *Aram,* used very indefinitely to include even Palestine, is in its proper sense applied to that region north of Mount Hermon and east of Phœnicia, to the desert on the east and Amanus Mountains on the north. The only point where it touches the Mediterranean is near the mouth of the Orontes. There are three divisions to this land. On the north it is AN ELEVATED PLATEAU, thinly inhabited. Between the *Anti-Lebanon and Lebanon Mountains* is COELE-SYRIA or *Hollow Syria,* with the *Orontes* flowing north in it and the

LYSTRA

TARSUS
Photo by W. H. Rau

MILETUS
Photo by W. H. Rau

EPHESUS
Photo by W. H. Rau

TROAS
Photo by Riley

PHILIPPI
Photo by W. H. Rau

ATHENS
General View
Photo by S. U. Mitman

ATHENS, MARS HILL
Photo by S. U. Mitman

Litany flowing south. The third section is the eastern level PLAIN OF DAMASCUS, of which we have spoken in dealing with the zone of Palestine, east of the Jordan. Among the important cities not treated before is *Carchemish*, on the upper Euphrates, the ruins of which are found at Jerablus now. It was for centuries the capital of the ancient Hittite kingdom. Another is *Antioch in Syria*, not to be confounded with the other Antioch in Pisidia (Asia Minor). S. Paul visited both of these towns.

It was captured by Pharaoh-Necho after the victory at Megiddo (608 B. C.), but Nebuchadnezzar retook it three years later. (2 Chron. 35 : 20; Jer. 46 : 2.) *Hamath* is on the Orontes, near the northern limits of Palestine. Its king sent presents to David when he defeated the king of Zobah. It is mentioned frequently in the Bible. (Look up Num. 13 : 21; 34 : 8; 2 Sam. 8 : 8; 2 Chron. 8 : 4; 2 Kings 14 : 28; 18 : 14; 19 : 13.) *Tadmor or Palmyra,* the City of Palms, is in an oasis about 150 miles from Damascus, northeast. It is mentioned, too, in the Bible and has now extensive ruins remaining. (2 Chron. 8 : 4; 1 Kings 9 : 18.) *Baalbec,* See opp. p. 53 the *City of Baal* or *City of the Sun,* the Greek *Heliopolis,* is in Coele-Syria, 35 miles from Damascus. There are wonderful ruins there to-day, two great temples and other buildings, often visited by travelers. *Riblah* is on the Orontes, 35 miles from Baalbec. Pharaoh-Necho and Nebuchadnezzar both had headquarters there. *Antioch, in Syria,* was founded about See opp. p. 53 300 B. C., and is located towards the mouth of the Orontes. It was the capital of Syria for a long period, and the third most important city in the Roman empire, coming next to Rome and Alexandria. It was here that the disciples were first called Christians. It was named Antioch the Beautiful and the Crown of the East. It is now a city of some 6,000 souls. *Seleucia,* at the mouth of this same river, was the Port of Antioch.

Questions and Manual Work on Chapter XI.

1. On your creased-paper outline map of the Eastern World, color in in crayons or water colors the kingdoms mentioned in this chapter.

2. Mark in and name the cities and places.

3. Color the Littlefield Historical Old Testament Maps ahead and note which kingdoms in order rose into power and waned.

CHAPTER XII

THE LANDS OF ST. PAUL'S LABORS.—ASIA MINOR, THE MEDITERRANEAN, GREECE, ROME

Asia Minor is the peninsula at the northwest corner of the Continent of Asia, jutting out towards Greece between the Mediterranean and the Black (Euxine) Seas. It was composed of some fourteen provinces (ten of which are mentioned in the New Testament), combined under the Roman government, politically, into seven. On the north *Bithynia* (Acts 16 : 7; 1 S. Peter 1 : 1), *Paphlagonia, and Pontus* (Acts 2 : 9; 18 : 2; 1 S. Peter 1 : 1) formed the Roman PROVINCE OF BITHYNIA AND PONTUS. To the west, *Mysia* (Acts 16 : 7, 8), *Lydia, Caria* and part of *Phrygia* formed the PROVINCE OF ASIA. When Asia is mentioned in the Bible it never means the Continent, but this Province. Southeast of Asia is *Lycia* (Acts 27 : 5) ; next comes *Pamphylia.* (Acts 13 : 13.) Then *the Kingdom of Antiochus,* then *Cilicia.* (Acts 6 : 9.) North of the Kingdom of Antiochus was *Cappadocia* (Acts 2 : 9), and in the very center was the large Province of *Galatia,* including Lycaonia. (Acts 14 : 1-23.) Excepting Jews and Jewish converts, all the inhabitants of this vast region of 156,000 square miles were idolaters, with many gods and many religions. Most of the people were Greek colonists; some were Romans, some Jews, and many native races. These latter lived chiefly outside of the large cities, which were occupied by Greeks, Romans, and Jews.

Looking at each province in order, we find that S. Paul did not enter BITHYNIA-PONTUS at all, though S. Peter in his First Epistle sends a greeting to Christians of Bithynia and of Pontus. He also does likewise for the Christians of CAPPADOCIA, some of whom heard him on the Day of Pentecost at Jerusalem. (Acts 1.) S. Paul did not visit this province either. GALATIA, as a province, included *Galatia* proper, a region settled by Gauls about 300 B. C., and *South Galatia*, composed of *Lycaonia, Pisidia,* and part of *Phrygia. Ancyra* was the capital of the whole province. It is now called *Angora,* and was the source of the Angora goats.

See opp. p. 53 *Antioch* was the principal city of South Galatia, to be carefully distinguished from Antioch in Syria. This one was called Antioch towards Pisidia, though it was actually in Phrygia. S. Paul visited it, and found a goodly Jewish colony settled there. (Acts 13 : 14.)

Iconium, Lystra, and Derbe are other important cities, all of them visited by S. Paul in his several missionary journeys.

See opp. p. 56 It was at *Lystra* that the citizens thought S. Paul and S. Barnabas were gods and tried to worship them. The uncertainty of the use of the name "Galatia," whether intending to designate simply the northern portion of the Province or the whole of it, has given rise to the controversy as to the Epistle to the Galatians, written by S. Paul. The general view to-day, called the South Galatian View, is that it was intended for the Christians of *Lystra, Derbe, Iconium, and Antioch,* and that S. Paul never visited the northern district

See opp. p. 56 at all. In CILICIA, *Tarsus* was the principal city, and was famous for being the birthplace of S. Paul. In LYCIA, *Myra,* the capital, was three miles from the mouth of a river. S. Paul stopped there on the last voyage to Rome. (Acts 27 : 5.) *Patara* was near the mouth of the *River Xanthus,* an important commercial city, devoted to the worship of Apollo. (Acts 21 : 1.) S. Paul also stopped there. ASIA was the largest of the Provinces of Asia Minor, and the most im-

See opp. p. 56 portant. In the subdivision, Caria, was the town of *Miletus,* one of the leading Ionian cities. Messengers were sent to this town by S. Paul. (Acts 20 : 15-17.) In the Lydia sub-

See opp. p. 56 division is *Ephesus,* the capital of the province, and the greatest trade center of that region, owing to its fine harbor. Here was centered the worship of Diana, the Roman equivalent of the Greek Artemis. A rich business in making silver shrines of the goddess was carried on in this town. (Acts 19 : 24.) S. Paul spent much time and wrought great results here. Smyrna, forty miles from Ephesus, had as its chief

CORINTH, MODERN
Photo by Williams, Brown & Earle

CORINTH, OLD
Photo by W. H. Rau

CENCHREA
Photo by W. H. Rau

MITYLENE
Photo by W. H. Rau

ISLAND OF PATMOS
Photo by Williams, Brown & Earle

MALTA
Photo by Williams, Brown & Earle

SYRACUSE
Photo by W. H. Rau

RHEGIUM
Photo by Williams, Brown & Earle

gods, Nemesis and Dionysus, the god of wine. Ignatius, the Christian Bishop of Smyrna, was thrown to wild beasts and met his death as a martyr in the amphitheater here, and here also Bishop Polycarp, a disciple of S. John, was burned at the stake. *Sardis, Philadelphia,* and *Thyatira* are other cities of this same district, the former noted for its dyers' guilds (Acts 16 : 14) and both mentioned in the letters to the Seven Churches in Revelation, Chapters 2 and 3.

In the Phrygia district are *Laodicaea* and *Colosse,* cities which S. Paul does not seem to have visited; but which are mentioned in his writings. (See Acts 20 : 17; 21 : 1; Col. 4 : 9, 12, 16, 17.) They may have been founded by S. Paul's helpers, while he was laboring at Ephesus. *Colosse* was the home of Philemon, Onesimus, and Epaphras. *Pergamos,* in MYSIA, is said, at one time, to have been the most beautiful city in all Asia Minor. It had a magnificent temple to Aphrodite and another to Esculapius. *Troas* was another See opp. p. 57 important city of the same district, situated on the Aegean Sea.

We now cross over to **Greece.** All the places visited by S. Paul and his co-workers in this section are included in Achaia and **Macedonia,** provinces of the Roman Empire. ACHAIA was the Roman name for the little land of Greece, the ruling state of which was Achaia, from which the name was applied to the whole region. MACEDONIA was the district north of Achaia, famous for its mighty kings, Philip of Macedon and Alexander the Great. Crossing from Troas, in Mysia, S. Paul went first to *Philippi* (Acts 16 : 12-40), See opp. p. 57 named after Philip, the father of Alexander. Near it was fought the world-battle between Augustus and Antony, and Brutus and Cassius, which crushed the hope of a Roman republic and began the empire. It was a Roman colony and its rulers bore Roman titles. Here Lydia the first European convert was baptized, a church was founded, S. Paul and Silas were scourged, a jailer was converted to Christianity, and much people brought to the Master. (See Acts 16 : 3, 9-12; 1 Thess. 1 : 7, 8.) It was called the Chief City of Macedonia in the Book of Acts. *Neapolis* was the port of Philippi. *Amphipolis* was 33 miles southwest of Philippi, three miles from the sea. In S. Paul's time, it had started on the wane, having no synagogue and few, if any, Jews. He tarried there but a day. (Acts 17 : 1.) *Thessalonica* was the capital of the whole province. It was forty miles from Amphipolis. It had a synagogue and many Jews dwelt there. S. Paul founded there a Church of Gentiles, and wrote two Epistles to them. The people stirred up a riot and expelled the Apostles from the city. At the present day, under the name *Saloniki,* it ranks as the second city of European Turkey, with a population of 80,000 persons. (See Acts 17 : 1-9; 1 Thess. 1 : 7, 8.) *Berea* (Acts 17 : 10-13), thirty-five miles from the preceding, was a small city, selected by S. Paul because of its retirement. Its inhabitants accepted the Gospel gladly, giving eager attention to its preachment. In fact the title Berean has stood as a synonym for faithful Bible students ever since.

See opp. p. 57 In ACHAIA OR GREECE, *Athens* was the most famous city of all the world. (Acts 17 : 15-34.) It was situated on a jutting promontory on the south, surrounded by noted mountains, and See opp. p. 57 itself cut up in the center by four hills; the Acropolis, surmounted by the Parthenon; the Areopagus, where S. Paul preached his startling sermon; the Pnyx; and the Museum. In S. Paul's time, Athens, though not the political center, was still the literary focus of the Empire. No church appears to have been founded by S. Paul, as the outcome of this sermon; but four centuries later, that very Parthenon became a Christian church and the Athenians the most hostile foes of image worship. It had been the chief city of images and shrines before. All the gods were honored, Apollo, Zeus, Bacchus, Mercury, etc., all had temples. On Mars' Hill, the Areopagus met, the famous Council or Court, from which the hill was named. In the Parthenon, the temple of Pallas, was the great statue of ivory and gold made by Phidias.

See opp. p. 60 *Corinth* was at the middle of the Grecian Isthmus, with two Ports, east and west, *Cenchreae* and *Lechaeum.* (Acts See opp. p. 60 18 : 1-18.) It was forty miles from Athens. *The Isthmus* is here 10 miles wide. It was the residence of the Proconsul and the commercial and political center of Greece. A very wicked and licentious city it was, and near it were celebrated the Isthmian games. S. Paul preached in Corinth a year and a half, working at his trade of tent-making. Here he wrote the two Epistles to the Thessalonians. After he left Corinth, he addressed the Corinthians two Epistles. During the wars with Rome, Corinth was utterly sacked and destroyed. For a century it lay in ruins. Then it was rebuilt and became a Roman colony. Now only a tiny village marks its desolate site. *Cenchreae* (Acts 18 : 18) was the city where S. Paul See opp. p. 60 cut off his hair in the Levitical vow and established a Church (Rom. 16 : 1, 2) and had a deaconess there, named Phebe.

There are several Islands of importance in Bible history. Some are in the AEGEAN SEA and some in the MEDITERRANEAN. In the AEGEAN SEA, we have, beginning at the northern end, *Samothracia,* a small but lofty island; *Mitylene or Lesbos,* See opp. p. 60 famous as the home of the Greek poetess, Sappho (Acts 26 : 14); *Chios,* another island, said to have been the birth-place of Homer (Acts 20 : 15); *Samos,* the birthplace of Pythagoras, the philosopher (Acts 20 : 15); *Patmos,* twenty See opp. p. 6 miles south of Samos, was the island of S. John's apocalyptic vision recorded in the Book of Revelation. *Trogyllium,* a town or cape on Asia Minor, the anchorage of S. Paul's party, still called *"S. Paul's Port"* (Acts 20 : 15); *Coos,* now called *Stanchio* (Acts 21 : 1) and, in the MEDITERRANEAN, *Rhodes,* an island of note, 46 miles long and 18 miles wide, where the figure of Colossus stood, 100 feet high, overthrown by an earthquake and so prostrate at S. Paul's visit (Acts 21 : 1); *Cyprus,* named from its rich copper mines (Greek, Kupros, copper), spoken of in the Old Testament as Chittim (Isa. 23 : 12), whose favorite goddess was Aphrodite, the birth-place of S. Barnabas, governed when S. Paul passed it (Acts 27 : 4) by a proconsul, ruling over four large cities, *Paphos, Salamis, Amathus,* and *Citium; Crete or Candia,* at the en-trance of the Aegean Sea, an island with an area of 3,300 square miles, with 100 cities to its credit (Acts 2 : 11), among which was *Fair Havens,* where S. Paul's vessel touched for anchorage and temporary safety (Acts 27 : 7-13), (over this island, S. Titus ruled as Bishop (Titus 1 : 5) a little later; *Malta,* the ancient *Melita,* now under British rule, on which See opp. p. 61 island the vessel was shipwrecked (Acts 28 : 7) and where the prisoners stayed all winter, setting sail for Rome in the spring.

Italy is our only remaining, untraversed Bible land.
At its foot was the great island of SICILY. On the last Voyage See opp. p. 61 to Rome, S. Paul stopped at *Syracuse,* on the eastern shore. See opp. p. 61 (Acts 28 : 12.) The next important town is *Rhegium,* at the toe of the Italian boot, now the flourishing town of *Rheggio.* (Acts 28 : 13.) Half-way up the Italian coast towards Rome is *Puteoli,* near Naples, one of the leading ports of Italy, being to Rome what Liverpool is to London. Here S. Paul found a Christian Church and remained See opp. p. 64 a week. The city is now *Pòzzuoli.* At a place, called *Appii* See opp. p. 64 *Forum,* the Forum of Appius, *the Appian Way,* 43 miles from Rome, and again at *Three Taverns,* 10 miles on, S. Paul stopped, met Christians, and received a welcome. (Acts See opp. p. 64 28 : 15.) *Rome* stands on the river Tiber. In its glory it spread over ten hills, though tradition says it was founded on seven. Here S. Paul remained in prison. Here some See opp. p. 64 years later, he and S. Peter suffered martyrdom. S. Paul was imprisoned in his own hired house near the Pretorian Camp, while the Jewish Quarter was on the opposite side of the City. At this time, Rome had about 1,200,000 inhabitants, one-half of whom were slaves, and two-thirds of the rest paupers, supported by free food from the rich. In Rome, S. Paul wrote the Epistles to the Ephesians, Colossians, Philippians, and Philemon. After two years he was released, and probably spent two years or more in preaching before his final imprisonment and death.

Questions and Manual Work on Chapter XII.

1. Draw a map of Asia Minor giving every Province and District, i.e. noting those absorbed by the Roman Empire into a few provinces.

2. Locate the cities visited by S. Paul and the events noted at each.

3. Locate the remaining cities of importance not visited by S. Paul, using a different color for marking.

4. Draw a separate map of Greece and locate the cities and events.

POZZUOLI
Photo by W. H. Rau

APPIAN WAY
Photo by W. H. Rau

PALACE OF THE CAESARS
Rome

COLISEUM
Copyrighted by Underwood & Underwood

5. Take a Bailey Map of Roman World and locate all the islands, and make mention of events.

6. Do the same with Italy.

7. Take four such maps and from the key maps in the Appendix reproduce each of S. Paul's four journeys.

APPENDIX

HISTORICAL AND GEOGRAPHICAL MAPS OF THE OLD
AND NEW TESTAMENT AND JOURNEY
MAPS OF THE LIFE OF OUR LORD

KEY TO THE LOCATION OF EVENTS IN OUR LORD'S LIFE AS NOTED ON THE JOURNEY MAPS FOLLOWING

MAP NO. 21—THE THIRTY YEARS OF PRIVATE LIFE.

1. From Nazareth to Bethlehem
     (a)   The Journey of Mary and Joseph
     (b)   The Birth of Jesus
2. To Jerusalem
     (a)   The Presentation
3. To Bethlehem
     (a)   The Visit of the Magi
4. To Egypt
5. To Nazareth
6. To Jerusalem and Return to Nazareth
     (a)   Jesus in the Temple
     (b)   Boyhood and Young Manhood of Jesus at Nazareth

MAP NO. 22—THE OPENING EVENTS.

1. From Nazareth to Bethabara
     (a)   The Baptism
2. To the Wilderness
     (a)   The Temptation
3. To Bethabara
     (a)   The Testimony of John, the First Disciple
4. To Cana
     (a)   The First Miracle

MAP NO. 23—THE EARLY JUDEAN MINISTRY.

1. From Cana to Capernaum
2. To Jerusalem
     (a)   The Cleansing of the Temple
     (b)   The Conversation with Nicodemus
     (c)   Preaching in Judea
3. To Sychar
     (a)   The Conversation with the Woman of Samaria
4. To Galilee

MAP NO. 24—THE GALILEAN MINISTRY, FIRST PERIOD.

1. At Cana
     (a)   The Healing of the Nobleman's Son

4. To Bethsaida Julias
    (a) The First Rejection
5. To Capernaum
    (a) The Call of the Four Disciples
    (b) A Day of Miracles
4. The First Preaching Tour
    (a) A Leper Healed
5. To Capernaum
    (a) The Healing of the Paralytic
    (b) The Call of Matthew
6. To Jerusalem
    (a) The Healing at the Pool of Bethesda
7. Return to Galilee
    (a) The Sabbath Question on the Way

MAP NO. 25—THE GALILEAN MINISTRY, SECOND PERIOD

1. At the Mount of Beatitudes
    (a) The Twelve Chosen
    (b) The Sermon on the Mount
2. To Capernaum
    (a) The Healing of the Centurion's Servant
3. The Second Preaching Tour
    (a) The Widow's Son Restored
    (b) The Messengers from John
    (c) The Feast in the House of Simon
4. To Capernaum
    (a) The Parables by the Sea
5. To Kersa
    (a) The Stilling of the Tempest
    (b) The Healing of the Demoniacs
6. To Capernaum
    (a) Four Miracles
7. The Third Preaching Tour
    (a) The Second Rejection at Nazareth
    (b) The Mission of the Twelve
    (c) The Death of John
8. To the Lakeside and Capernaum
    (a) Feeding the 5,000
    (b) Walking on the Sea
    (c) The Crisis in Capernaum

MAP NO. 26—THE GALILEAN MINISTRY, THIRD PERIOD

1. From Capernaum to Phoenicia
    (a) The Heathen Woman's Daughter Healed
2. To Decapolis
    (a) A Stammerer and Many Sick Healed
    (b) The Feeding of the 4,000

3. To Dalmanutha
    (a) A Sign Demanded
2. To Nazareth
    (a) A Blind Man Healed
5. To Caesarea Philippi
    (a) Peter's Confession
6. To Mt. Hermon
    (a) The Tranfiguration
    (b) The Demoniac Boy Healed
7. To Capernaum
    (a) The Shekel in the Fish's Mouth
    (b) The Child in the Midst
8. To Jerusalem
    (a) At the Feast of Tabernacles
9. Return to Capernaum

MAP NO. 27—THE PEREAN MINISTRY.

1. The Final Departure from Galilee
    (a) The Mission of the Seventy
    (b) The Good Samaritan
    (c) Rejected by the Samaritans' Village
2. To Bethany
    (a) A Visit to Mary and Martha
3. To Jerusalem
    (a) The Healing of the Man Born Blind
    (b) The Good Shepherd
    (c) The Feast of Dedication
4. Through Perea
    (a) Teaching and Healing
    (b) The Parables of Luke 15
5. To Bethany
    (a) The Raising of Lazarus
6. The Withdrawal to Ephraim
7. Through Samaria, Galilee, and Perea
    (a) The Ten Lepers
    (b) The Pharisee and the Publican
    (c) Blessing the Children
    (d) The Rich Young Ruler
8. To Jericho
    (a) Two Blind Men Healed
    (b) The Visit to Zacchaeus
9. To Bethany
    (a) The Anointing by Mary

MAP NO. 28—THE APPEARANCES OF THE FORTY DAYS

1, 2. At Jerusalem
    (a) To Mary
    (b) To the Women

3. On the Emmanus Road
     (a)   To Two
4, 5, 6.   At Jerusalem
     (a)   To Peter
     (b)   To Ten
     (c)   To Eleven
7. On the Lake Side
     (a)   To Seven
8. On a Mountain in Galilee
     (a)   The Great Commission
9. At Jerusalem
     (a)   To James
10. Near Bethany
     (a)   The Ascension

THE JOURNEYS AND PRINCIPAL EVENTS IN APOSTOLIC HISTORY

MAP NO. 29—PHILIP'S JOURNEY

(Acts 8)

1. From Jerusalem to Samaria
     (a)   Driven from Jerusalem by Persecution
     (b)   Established a Church at Samaria
2. Toward Gaza
     (a)   The Conversion of the Ethiopian
3. To Azotus
4. To Caesarea
     (a)   Through the Cities of the Maritime Plain
     (b)   Prepared the Way for the Establishing of Churches in Lydda, Joppa, and Caesarea

MAP NO. 30—SAUL'S JOURNEY

(Acts 9)

1. From Jerusalem to Damascus
     (a)   Conversion by the Way
2. To Arabia
     (a)   In Retirement for Three Years
3. Return to Damascus
     (a)   Preached in the Synagogue
4. To Jerusalem
     (a)   Distrusted at First
     (b)   Commended by the Church of Barnabas
5. To Tarsus
     (a)   In Retirement for Three or Four Years

MAP NO. 31—S. PETER'S JOURNEY

(Acts 9 : 32 to 11 : 2)

1. From Jerusalem to Lydda
     (a) The Healing of Aeneas
2. To Joppa
     (a) The Raising of Dorcas
     (b) The Vision on the Housetop
3. To Caesarea
     (a) The Conversion of the House of Cornelius
4. Return to Jerusalem

MAP NO. 32—JOURNEYS OF S. BARNABAS AND S. PAUL

(Acts 11 : 19-28)

1. Barnabas to Antioch
     (a) To Direct the New Work at Antioch
2. To Tarsus for S. Paul
3. S. Barnabas and S. Paul to Antioch
     (a) Established the First Gentile Church
     (b) The First to be Called "Christian"
     (c) The First to Send Missionaries to the Heathen
          World
4. S. Barnabas and S. Paul to Jerusalem
     (a) To Carry Reports of the Work Among the
          Gentiles
     (b) And to take an Offering for the Poor of Jeru-
          salem in the time of Famine
     (c) S. Peter Imprisoned and Delivered by an Angel
5. Return of S. Barnabas and S. Paul to Antioch

MAP NO. 33—S. PAUL'S FIRST MISSIONARY JOURNEY

(Acts 13 and 14)

1. At Antioch
2. To Salamis
     (a) Preached to the Jews
3. To Paphos
     (a) Sergius Paulus Converted
4. To Perga
     (a) Desertion of Mark
5. To Antioch in Galatia
     (a) Disciples Made
     (b) Persecution
     (c) S. Paul Ill
6. To Iconium
     (a) Disciples Made
     (b) Persecution

7. To Lystra
    (a)   Disciples Made
    (b)   Stoned
8. To Derbe
    (a)   Disciples Made
    (b)   Return Home by the Same Route
9. To Attalia
    (a)   Took Ship for Home
10. To Antioch
    (a)   Opposition to S. Paul

MAP NO. 34—S. PAUL'S SECOND MISSIONARY JOURNEY
(Acts 15 : 36 to 18 : 22)

1. At Antioch
    (a)   Refusal to take Mark
    (b)   Joined by Silas
2. To Lystra
    (a)   Joined by Timothy
3. To Troas
    (a)   Vision and Call to Macedonia
4. To Philipp
    (a)   Lydia and Others Converted
    (b)   Imprisoned and Released
5. To Thessalonica
    (a)   Disciples Made
    (b)   Persecution and Arrest
6. To Beroea
    (a)   Disciples Made
    (b)   Persecution
7. To Athens
    (a)   The Altar to the Unknown God
8. To Corinth
    (a)   Disciples Made
    (b)   1 and 2 Thessalonians Written
9. To Ephesus
    (a)   Disciples Made
10. To Jerusalem
    (a)   Reported His Work
11. To Antioch

MAP NO. 35—S. PAUL'S THIRD MISSIONARY JOURNEY
(Acts 18 : 23 to 23 : 35)

1. At Antioch
2. Through Phrygia and Galatia
3. To Ephesus Three Years
    (a)   Converts Made
    (b)   1 Corinthians Written
    (c)   2 Corinthians Written
    (d)   Burning of Pagan Books and Riot

4. To Macedonia
    (a)   Collections in the Macedonian Churches for the Poor of Judea
5. To Corinth Three Months
    (a)   1 Timothy and Titus Written
    (b)   Romans Written
    (c)   Plot Against S. Paul
6. To Troas
    (a)   Accident to Eutychus
7. To Miletus
    (a)   Farewell to the Ephesians
8. To Tyre and Ptolemais
    (a)   Conferences with the Disciples
9. To Jerusalem
    (a)   Riot in the Temple
    (b)   Arrest of S. Paul
    (c)   Defense Before the People and the Sanhedrin
    (d)   Plot Against S. Paul, taken to Caesarea

MAP NO. 36—S. PAUL'S VOYAGE TO ROME

(Acts 27 and 28)

1. At Caesarea
    (a)   Defense Before Felix and Agrippa
    (b)   S. Paul's Appeal to Caesar, Acts 24 and 26
2. To Sidon
    (a)   The Church Greeted
3. To Myra
    (a)   Changed Ships
4. To Fair Havens
    (a)   Sailed for Phoenix
5. To Cauda
    (a)   Driven
6. To Melita
    (a)   Wrecked
    (b)   Entertained by Publius
    (c)   Miracles of Healing
7. To Puteoli
    (a)   Met by Christians
8. To Rome
    (a)   Imprisoned Two Years
    (b)   Sent for the Jews, Winning a Few
    (c)   Ephesians Written
    (d)   Colossians Written
    (e)   Philippians Written
    (f)   Philemon Written
    (g)   Released and Re-imprisoned
    (h)   2 Timothy Written
    (i)   Executed

MAP NO. I. THE WORLD ON MERCATOR PROJECTION, OUTLINE
Showing position and size of Palestine

MAP NO. 2. PHYSICAL MAP OF PALESTINE, RELIEF
(By permission of the Palestine Exploration Fund)
[The original of this map, mounted on rollers, may be obtained of the
N. Y. S. S. Commission, at $3.25. Postage 15 cents additional.]

WESTERN ASIA
(EARLY TIMES)

ENGLISH MILES
0   50   100   150   200   250

Copyright, 1893, by The Bible Study Publishing Company.

MAP NO. 3.   WESTERN ASIA IN EARLY TIMES, OUTLINE

CASPIAN Sea

MEDIA

ELAM

Mt. Ararat
17,000 ft.

ASSYRIA

R. Tigris

CHALDEA

Persian Gulf

Nineveh
Resen Calah

BABYLONIA

Accad

Babel Shinar

Calneh

Ur of Chaldees
(Mugheir)

Mesopotamia

Haran
(Padan Aram?)

R. Euphrates

Arabian Desert

Damascus

SYRIA

Hamath

Sidon

CANAAN

Shechem

Bethel

Hebron

Beer-sheba

KITTIM

THE GREAT

SEA

SINAI

EGYPT
OR
MIZRAIM

COPYRIGHT, 1895, BIBLE STUDY PUB. CO.

EGYPT, SINAI
AND
CANAAN.
Based on the most recent Information
English Miles

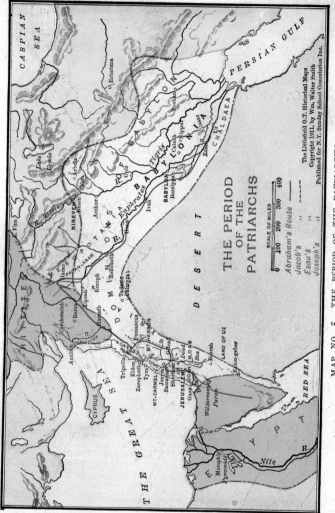

MAP NO. 5.   THE PERIOD OF THE PATRIARCHS

MAP NO. 6. ROUTE OF THE EXODUS

PERIOD OF THE
TRIBAL
SETTLEMENTS

SCALE OF MILES

0   10   20   30   40   50

The Littlefield O.T. Historical Maps
Copyright 1911, by Wm. Walter Smith
Published for N.Y. Sunday School Commission Inc.

MAP NO. 7.   PERIOD OF THE TRIBAL SETTLEMENTS.   APPROXIMATE,
ACCORDING TO BOOK OF JOSHUA

THE PERIOD OF
THE JUDGES
1270–1030

SCALE OF MILES
0   20   40   60   80   100

The Littlefield O.T. Historical Maps
Copyright 1911, by Wm. Walter Smith
Published for N. Y. Sunday School Commission. Inc.

MAP NO. 8.   PERIOD OF THE JUDGES, 1270–1030

THE KINGDOM
OF SAUL
1030-1010

SCALE OF MILES

0   20   40   60   80   100

The Littlefield O.T. Historical Maps
Copyright 1911, by Wm. Walter Smith
Published for N.Y. Sunday School Commission Inc.

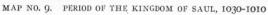

MAP NO. 9.   PERIOD OF THE KINGDOM OF SAUL, 1030-1010

ASSYRIANS

HITTITES

THE GREAT SEA

PHŒNICIANS

R. Orontes

R. Euphrates

Hamath

Tripolis

MT. HOR

Rehob

Sidon

MT. HERMON

R. Abanah

Damascus

Tyre

Dan

R. Pharpar

Achzib

Ramah

Waters of

Accho

Hazor

Meroth

Ptolemais

Sea of

Chinnereth

Great Syrian Desert

Tadmor

DOMINIONS

Jabneel

HILLS OF

MT. CARMEL

Daberath

Aphek

BASHAN

Dor

Ender

Shunem

R. Jarmuk

Edrei

Dothan

Tirzah

Jabesh-Gilead

Samaria

Ramath-Gilead

Shechem

Joppa

Shiloh

Jericho

Penuel

Gibeon

Geba

Beth-Peor

JERUSALEM

Nob

Heshbon

Kirjath-Jearim

MT. NEBO

Askelon

Bethlehem

Gaza

Eshcol

Hebron

Aroer

Brook Besor

Etam

Ziph

Salt

Gerar

Juttah

Ar

Sea

Beer-Sheba

Kir

THE NEGEB

HEBREWS

MT. HOR

Wilderness of Shur

Wilderness of Zin

Wilderness of Paran

Ezion-geber

Elath

Red Sea

THE EMPIRE OF
DAVID AND SOLOMON
1000-937

SCALE OF MILES

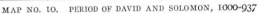

0   20   40   60   80   100

The Litfefield O.T. Historical Maps
Copyright 1911, by Wm. Walter Smith
Published for N. Y. Sunday School Commission, Inc.

MAP NO. 10.   PERIOD OF DAVID AND SOLOMON, 1000-937

ASSYRIANS

HITTITES

R. *Orontes*

THE GREAT SEA

Hamath

Tadmor

Tripolis

MT. HOR

Rehob

Great Syrian

Sidon
MT. HERMON
Abanah
R.
Damascus

Desert

Tyre
Luz
Dan
R. *Pharpar*
Achzib
Ramah
Waters of Merom
Ptolemais
Hazor

Sea of Chinnereth
Jabesh-Gilead
SHILLS OF
Aphek
BASHAN

MT. CARMEL
Endor
Shunem
R. *Yarmuk*
Edrei
Dor
Jabesh-Gilead
Dothan
Samaria
Shechem
Ramoth-Gilead
Joppa
Shiloh
Penuel
Succoth
Adam
AMMONITES
Gibeon
Jericho
Beth
Peor
Kirjath-Jearim
No
Heshbon
Askelon
Gath
Bethlehem
MT. NEBO
Gaza
Eshcol
Hebron
Gerar
Eshtam
Ziph
R. *Arnon*
Aroer
Gath
Juttah
Ar
Engedi
Salt
Sea
Beer-Sheba
Kir

THE NEGEB
MT. HOR
Wilderness
of Shur
Wilderness of Zin
DOMINIONS
OF
JUDAH

MOABITES

Wilderness of Paran

Ezion-geber
Elath

Red Sea

THE
DIVIDED KINGDOM
TO THE
REVOLUTION OF JEHU
937-842

SCALE OF MILES

0   20   40   60   80   100

The Littlefield O.T. Historical Maps
Copyright 1911, by Wm. Walter Smith
Published for N.Y. Sunday School Commission, Inc.

MAP NO. II.   DIVIDED KINGDOM TO REVOLUTION OF JEHU, 937-848

The following labels appear on the map:

ASSYRIANS

HITTITES

R.

Orontes

R. Euphrates

Hamath

DOMINIONS

Tadmor

THE GREAT SEA

PHŒNICIANS

Tripolis

MT. HOR

OF SYRIA

Rehob

Great Syrian

Sidon

MT. HERMON

R. Abanah

Damascus

Desert

Tyre

Ijon

Dan

R. Pharpar

Achzib

Luz

Ramah

Waters of

Accho

Hazor

Merom

Ptolemais

Sea of

Chinnereth

HILLS OF

Dabrath

Aphek

MT. CARMEL

Endor

BASHAN

Dor

Shunem

R. Yarmuk

Edrei

Dothan

Tirzah

Jabesh-Gilead

Samaria

MT.

Ramath-Gilead

Shechem

EBAL

AMMONITES

Joppa

Shiloh

Succoth

Penuel

Gibeon

Ai

Bethel

Beth Peor

Kirjath-Jearim

JERUSALEM

Jericho

Heshbon

Askelon

Gath

Sucoth

MT. NEBO

Gaza

Eshcol

Hebron

Bethlehem

R. Arnon

Gerar

Juttah

Ziph

Aroer

Brook Besor

Etam

Engedi

Ar

Salt

Shephelah

Sea

Kir

Beer-Sheba

THE NEGEB

MT. HOR

EDOMITES

MOABITES

Wilderness

Wilderness

of Shur

of Zin

Wilderness of Paran

Ezion-geber

Elath

Red

Sea

THE
SYRIAN CONQUESTS
IN THE
REIGN OF HAZAEL
About 814 to 797

SCALE OF MILES

0   20   40   60   80   100

The Litlefield O.T. Historical Maps
Copyright 1911, by Wm. Walter Smith
Published for N.Y. Sunday School Commission. Inc.

MAP NO. 12. SYRIAN CONQUESTS IN THE REIGN OF HAZAEL,
814-797

THE
SCYTHIAN INVASION
AND THE
PERIOD OF JOSIAH
628: 639-608

SCALE OF MILES
0   20   40   60   80   100

The Littlefield O.T. Historical Maps
Copyright 1911, by Wm. Walter Smith
Published for N.Y. Sunday School Commission. Inc.

MAP NO. 17. SCYTHIAN INVASION AND THE PERIOD OF JOSIAH,
639-608

MAP NO. 18.   BABYLONIAN PERIOD, 605-586

Map text includes:

DOMINIONS
OF ASSYRIA
R. Euphrates
R. Orontes
Hamath
Tadmor
Great Syrian
Desert
Tripolis
MT. HOR
Rehob
Sidon
MT. HERMON
Abanah
Damascus
R. Pharpar
Ijon
Dan
Tyre
Luz
Waters of
Merom
Achzib
Ramah
Accho
Ptolemais
Hazor
Sea of
Chinnereth
(Abbek)
HILLS OF
BASHAN
MT. CARMEL
Daberath
Endor
R. Jarmuk
Dor
Shunem
Edrei
Dothan
Tirzah
Jabesh-Gilead
Samaria
Ramoth-Gilead
Shechem
Adam
Joppa
Shiloh
Jericho
Penuel
AMMONITES
Gibeah
Gaza
Beth-Peor
JERUSALEM
Nob
Heshbon
Kirjath Jearim
Gath
Ekron
Askelon
Bethlehem
MT. NEBO
Gaza
Succoth
Hebron
R. Arnon
Brook Besor
Eshcol
Etam
Aroer
Gerar
Ziph
Ar
Kiriah
Zephar
Juttah
Salt
Kir
Beer-Sheba
Engedi
Sea
THE NEGEB
MT. HOR
MOABITES
Wilderness
of Shur
Wilderness
of Zin
EDOMITES
Wilderness of Paran
Ezion-geber
Elath
Red
Sea
THE GREAT SEA
LEBANON MTS

THE ASSYRIAN
CONQUEST OF SYRIA
797-783

SCALE OF MILES
0   20   40   60   80   100

The Litlefield O.T. Historical Maps
Copyright 1911, by Wm. Walter Smith
Published for N.Y. Sunday School Commission, Inc.

MAP NO. 13. ASSYRIAN CONQUESTS OF SYRIA, 797-783

THE PERIOD
OF JEROBOAM II
780-740

SCALE OF MILES
0   20   40   60   80   100

The Littlefield O.T. Historical Maps
Copyright 1911, by Wm. Walter Smith
Published for N.Y. Sunday School Commission. Inc.

MAP NO. 14.   PERIOD OF JEROBOAM, 780-740

DOMINIONS OF

R. Euphrates

Hamath

ASSYRIA

Tadmor

THE GREAT SEA

PHOENICIANS

Tripoli

MT. HOR

Rehob

Sidon

Great Syrian

MT. HERMON

R. Abanah

Ijon

Damascus

Desert

Tyre

Dan

R. Pharpar

Achzib

Ramah

Waters of

Accho

Hazor

Meron

Ptolemais

Sea of

Taberath

Chinnereth

HILLS OF

MT. CARMEL

Endor

Aphek

BASHAN

Dor

Shunem

R. Yarmuk

Edrei

Dothan

Tirzah

Jabesh-Gilead

Samaria

Ramoth-Gilead

Shechem

ISRAEL

Joppa

Shiloh

AMMONITES

Succoth

Lydda

Jericho

Gibeon

Beth-Peor

Kirjath-Jearim

JERUSALEM

Nob

Heshbon

Askelon

Succoh

Bethlehem

MT. NEBO

Gaza

Eshcol

Hebron

R. Arnon

Brook Besor

Etam

Aroer

Ziph

Salt

Ar

Sepher

Juttah

Sea

Kir

Beer-sheba

Engedi

THE NEGEB

MT. HOR

MOABITES

Wilderness
of Shur

Wilderness
of Zin

EDOMITES

Wilderness of Paran

THE
CONQUESTS OF
TIGLATH-PILESER III
733-727

Ezion-geber

Elath

SCALE OF MILES

0 20 40 60 80 100

Red
Sea

The Littlefield O.T. Historical Maps
Copyright 1911, by Wm. Walter Smith
Published for N.Y. Sunday School Commission Inc.

MAP NO. 15. CONQUESTS OF TIGLATH-PILESER III, 733-727

THE
FALL OF ISRAEL
AND THE
PERIOD OF HEZEKIAH
721: 727-695

SCALE OF MILES
0   20   40   60   80   100

The Littlefield O.T. Historical Maps
Copyright 1911, by Wm. Walter Smith
Published for N.Y. Sunday School Commission Inc.

MAP NO. 16. FALL OF ISRAEL AND THE PERIOD OF HEZEKIAH,
727-695

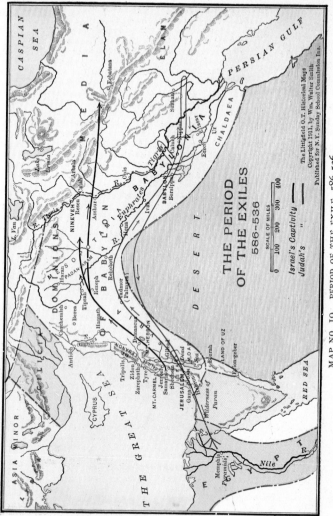

MAP NO. 19.   PERIOD OF THE EXILE, 586-536

THE PERIOD
OF THE EXILES
586-536

SCALE OF MILES
0   100   200   300   400

Israel's Captivity
Judah's   "

The Littlefield O.T. Historical Maps
Copyright 1911, by Wm. Walter Smith.
Published for N.Y. Sunday School Commission Inc.

THE
'PERSIAN PERIOD
536-332

SCALE OF MILES
0   20   40   60   80   100

The Littlefield O.T. Historical Maps
Copyright 1911, by Wm. Walter Smith
Published for N.Y. Sunday School Commission. Inc.

MAP NO. 20.   PERSIAN PERIOD, 536-332

MAP NO. 21.   THE THIRTY YEARS OF PRIVATE LIFE OF OUR LORD

PALESTINE
IN THE
TIME OF CHRIST

SCALE OF MILES

0   10   20   30

MEDITERRANEAN SEA

Sidon

Sarepta

DAMASCUS

Pharpar R.

ABILENE

LEBANON MTS.

LEONTES

TYRE

PHŒNICIA

Cæsarea Philippi

MT. HERMON

SYRIA

Kadesh
Hazor

HULEH

MEROM

GAULANITIS

ITUREA

Ptolemais

Zebulon

Chorazin

Bethsaida Julias

Bethsaida

DECAPOLIS

Capernaum

GALILEE

Magdala

SEA OF GALILEE

Geresa

AURANITIS

Tiberias

Hippos

Mt. Carmel

NAZARETH

Cana

Hieromax R.

TRACHONITIS

R. Kishon

Mt. Tabor

Gadara

Abila

Nain

BATANEA

Dora

Arbela

Scythopolis

Bethabara ?

CÆSAREA

Pella

SAMARIA

PLAIN OF SHARON

Gerasa

Samaria

Ænon

Sychar

Shechem

Salim

JORDAN R.

Jabbok R.

Shiloh

Antipatris

JOPPA

Ephraim

Phasaelis

Bethel

Philadelphia

Lydda

Modin

Mt. Quarantania

Bethabara ?

JAMNIA

JERICHO

PEREA

Adasa

JUDEA

Heshbon

JERUSALEM

BETHANY

Azotus

Emmaus

BETHLEHEM

Herodium

R. ARNON

ASCALON

THE

Machærus

DEAD

HEBRON

IDUMEA WILDERNESS

SEA

GAZA

Engedi

Arnon R.

GERAR

Juttah

GERARITICA

ARABIA

BEERSHEBA

The Littlefield Journey Maps
Copyright 1910, by Wm. Walter Smith
Published for N.Y. Sunday School Commission Inc.

MASADA

MAP NO. 22.   THE OPENING EVENTS OF CHRIST'S LIFE

PALESTINE
IN THE
TIME OF CHRIST

SCALE OF MILES

0   10   20   30

Sidon
Sarepta
TYRE
PHŒNICIA
LEBANON MTS.
LEONTES
ABILENE
MT. HERMON
DAMASCUS
Pharpar R.
SYRIA
Cæsarea Philippi
Kadesh
Hazor
LAULEH (MEROM)
GAULAN
ITUREA
Ptolemais
Zebulon
Chorazin
Capernaum
Bethsaida Julias
Bethsaida
DECAPOLIS
GALILEE
Magdala
SEA OF GALILEE
Geresa
AURANITIS
Tiberias
Hippos
R. NAZARETH
Cana
MT. CARMEL
R. Kishon
Mt. Tabor
Nain
Hieromax R.
Abila
TRACHONITIS
Gadara
Dora
BATANEA
Arbela
CÆSAREA
Scythopolis
Bethabara?
DECAPOLIS
Pella
SAMARIA
Gerasa
PLAIN OF SHARON
Samaria
Ænon
Sychar
Salim
Jabbok R.
Shechem
Antipatris
Shiloh
PEREA
JOPPA
Ephraim
Phasaelis
JORDAN R.
Lydda
Bethel
Mt. Quarantania
Philadelphia
JAMNIA
Modin
JERICHO
Bethabara?
Adasa
Azotus
JERUSALEM
BETHANY
Heshbon
Emmaus
BETHLEHEM
THE
JUDEA
Herodium
DEAD
ASCALON
HEBRON
Machærus
SEA
GAZA
IDUMEA WILDERNESS
Juttah
Engedi
Arnon R.
ARABIA
GERAR
GERARITICA
BEERSHEBA
MASADA

The Littlefield Journey Maps
Copyright 1910, by Wm. Walter Smith
Published for N.Y. Sunday School Commission Inc.

MEDITERRANEAN SEA

MAP NO. 23.   THE EARLY JUDEAN MINISTRY

PALESTINE
IN THE
TIME OF CHRIST

SCALE OF MILES
0   10   20   30

The Littlefield Journey Maps
Copyright 1910, by Wm. Walter Smith
Published for N.Y. Sunday School Commission Inc.

MAP NO. 24.   THE GALILEAN MINISTRY, FIRST PERIOD

PALESTINE
IN THE
TIME OF CHRIST

SCALE OF MILES
0   10   20   30

Sidon

PHŒNICIA   SYRIA

Sarepta   DAMASCUS

LEONTES   Pharpar R.

TYRE   Cæsarea Philippi

ABILENE   MT. HERMON

Kadesh   L. HULEH
Hazor   (MEROM)

ITUREA

MEDITERRANEAN SEA

Ptolemais   Zebulon   Chorazin   Bethsaida Julias
                   Capernaum   Bethsaida
GALILEE   Magdala   Gerasa   AURANITIS
L. NAZARETH   Tiberias   Hippos   DECAPOLIS
Kishon Cana   L. of GALILEE
Mt. Tabor   Hieromax R.   Abila   TRACHONITIS
Nain   Gadara
Dora   BATANEA   Arbela
CÆSAREA   Bethabara?
          Scythopolis

SAMARIA   Pella

PLAIN OF SHARON

Samaria   Ænon   Gerasa
Shechem   Sychar
                 Salim   Jabbok R.
Antipatris   Shiloh

JOPPA   Ephraim
Lydda   Bethel   Phasaelis
JAMNIA   Modin   Mt. Quarantania   Philadelphia
                 Adasa   JERICHO   Bethabara?
JUDEA   JERUSALEM BETHANY
Azotus   Emmaus   JUDEA   Heshbon
                 BETHLEHEM
ASCALON   Herodium
                              THE
GAZA   HEBRON
                              DEAD   Machærus
GERAR
                 Juttah   SEA   Arnon R.
GERARITICA
                          IDUMEAN WILDERNESS Engedi
BEERSHEBA
          MASADA

PEREA   ARABIA

The Littlefield Journey Maps
Copyright 1910, by Wm. Walter Smith
Published for N.Y. Sunday School Commission Inc.

MAP NO. 25.   THE GALILEAN MINISTRY, SECOND PERIOD

PALESTINE
IN THE
TIME OF CHRIST

SCALE OF MILES

0   10   20   30

MEDITERRANEAN SEA

PHŒNICIA

LEBANON MTS.

ABILENE

SYRIA

DAMASCUS

MT. HERMON

Pharpar R.

Sidon

Sarepta

LEONTES

TYRE

Cæsarea Philippi

Kadesh
Hazor

UPPER
(MEROM)

ITUREA

Ptolemais

Zebulon

Chorazin
Capernaum

Bethsaida Julias

DECAPOLIS

GALILEE

Bethsaida

Magdala
Tiberias
Cana

Geresa
Hippos

AURANITIS

NAZARETH

Mt. Tabor

Hieromax R.

TRACHONITIS

Mt. Carmel

Kishon R.

Nain

Gadara

Abila

BATANEA

Dora

Bethabara?

Arbela

CÆSAREA

Scythopolis

Pella

PLAIN OF SHARON

SAMARIA

Gerasa

Samaria

Ænon
Sychar
Salim

Jabbak R.

Shechem

Antipatris

Shiloh

JOPPA

Ephraim
Bethel

Phasaelis

PEREA

Lydda

Modin

Mt. Quarantania

Philadelphia

JAMNIA

JERICHO
Adasa

Bethabara?

JUDEA

Heshbon

JERUSALEM

BETHANY

Azotus

Emmaus
BETHLEHEM
Herodium

Brook Kidron

THE

ASCALON

Machærus

GAZA

DEAD

GERAR

HEBRON

SEA

Arnon R.

Jottah

ENGEDI

GERARITICA

IDUMEA

WILDERNESS OF JUDEA

JORDAN R.

ARABIA

BEERSHEBA

MASADA

The Littlefield Journey Maps
Copyright 1910, by Wm. Walter Smith
Published for N.Y. Sunday School Commission Inc.

MAP NO. 26.   THE GALILEAN MINISTRY, THIRD PERIOD

PALESTINE
IN THE
TIME OF CHRIST

SCALE OF MILES
0   10   20   30

The Littlefield Journey Maps
Copyright 1910, by Wm. Walter Smith
Published for N.Y. Sunday School Commission Inc.

MAP NO. 27. THE PEREAN MINISTRY

Sidon

Sarepta

TYRE

Ptolemais

SYRIA
DAMASCUS
Pharpar R.

PHŒNICIA
LEONTES
LEBANON MTS.
ABILENE
MT. HERMON

Cæsarea Philippi

Kadesh
Hazor
L. HULEH
(MEROM)

ITUREA

Zebulon
Chorazin
Capernaum
Bethsaida Julias
Bethsaida
GALILEE
Magdala
Tiberias
Cana
NAZARETH
Mt. Carmel
Kishon R.
Nain
Mt. Tabor

SEA OF GALILEE
Geresa
Hippos
Gadara
Arbela
Bethabara ?

AURANITIS
Hieromax R.
TRACHONITIS
Abila
BATANEA

DECAPOLIS

Dora
CÆSAREA
Scythopolis
Pella

MEDITERRANEAN SEA

PLAIN OF SHARON

SAMARIA
Samaria
Shechem
Ænon
Sychar
Salim
Shiloh

Gerasa

Jabbok R.

Antipatris

JOPPA
Lydda
JAMNIA
Azotus
ASCALON
GAZA
GERAR
GERARITICA
BEERSHEBA

Ephraim
Bethel
Modin
JERICHO
Adasa
JERUSALEM
Emmaus
BETHLEHEM
Herodium
Bethany

Phasælis
Mt. Quarantania

JUDEA

JORDAN R.

Philadelphia
Bethabara ?
Heshbon

PEREA

Brook Kidron
THE
DEAD
SEA
Machærus
Arnon R.

HEBRON
Juttah
Engedi
MASADA

WILDERNESS OF JUDEA
IDUMEA

ARABIA

MAP NO. 28.   THE APPEARANCES OF THE FORTY DAYS

THE PROVINCES
OF
SYRIA AND PALESTINE

SCALE OF MILES

0 10 20   40   60   80

The Littlefield Journey Maps
Copyright 1910, by Wm. Walter Smith.
Published for N.Y. Sunday School Commission Inc.

MAP NO. 29. S. PHILIP'S JOURNEY

The labels on the map include:

CAPPADOCIA · CILICIA · SYRIA · MESOPOTAMIA

Tarsus · GULF OF ISSUS · AMANUS MTS. · Euphrates R.

Seleucia · Antioch · Aleppo · Tiphsah

Apamea · Epiphania · Emesa · Palmyra

CYPRUS · Salamis · Tripolis · MEDITERRANEAN SEA

Chalcis · ANTI LIBANUS MTS. · DAMASCUS

Sidon · PHOENICIA · TYRE · Ptolemais · GALILEE · ITUREA · TRACHONITIS

SEA OF GALILEE · NAZARETH · Dora · PEREA

CÆSAREA · SAMARIA · Samaria · JOPPA · PALESTINE · Lydda · JAMNIA · Azotus · JERUSALEM · BETHLEHEM · THE DEAD SEA · GAZA · JUDEA

THE PROVINCES
OF
SYRIA AND PALESTINE

SCALE OF MILES

0 10 20   40   60   80

The Littlefield Journey Maps
Copyright 1910, by Wm. Walter Smith.
Published for N.Y. Sunday School Commission Inc.

MAP NO. 30.   SAUL'S JOURNEY

JERUSALEM
in the days of
NEHEMIAH
and at the time of the
GOSPELS.

SCALE OF ENGLISH FEET

0   500   1000   1500   2000   2500

Jeremiah's
Grotto
Calvary?

Pool of Bethesda

BEZETHA

Damascus Gate

Hananeel
Tower
Antonia
Meah Tower

St. Stephen's
Gate

Via Dolorosa

Herod's
Sheep
Gate

Extension

Golden
Gate.

Gethsemane

CHRISTIAN QUARTER

Church
of the
Sepulchre

Sanhedrin
Hall

Temple

Mosque of Omar

Solomon's Porch

Jaffa Gate

David Street

Robinson's
Arch

Horse Gate

Tower of
Herod

JEWISH QUARTER

Mills

Water Gate

Garden of Herod

ARMENIAN QUARTER

Gihon

House of Caiaphas

Traditional
Tomb of David

Siloam

Dung Gate

Dung Gate

PROBABLE HOUSE OF NEHEMIAH'S NIGHT RIDE

BURKAY & CO., N.Y.

MAP NO. 39.   JERUSALEM IN NEHEMIAH'S TIME, OUTLINE

MAP NO. 40. MODERN JERUSALEM

THE PROVINCES
OF
SYRIA AND PALESTINE

SCALE OF MILES

0   10 20   40   60   80

The Littlefield Journey Maps
Copyright 1910, by Wm. Walter Smith.
Published for N.Y. Sunday School Commission Inc.

MAP NO. 31.   S. PETER'S JOURNEY

THE PROVINCES
OF
SYRIA AND PALESTINE
SCALE OF MILES
0 10 20   40   60   80
The Littlefield Journey Maps
Copyright 1910, by Wm. Walter Smith.
Published for N.Y. Sunday School Commission Inc.

MAP NO. *32*.   JOURNEYS OF S. BARABAS AND S. PAUL

PALESTINE
SHOWING THE
PRINCIPAL ROADS
IN THE
TIME OF CHRIST

Sidon

SYRIA

PHŒNICIA

Damascus

Tyre

Cæsarea Philippi

GALILEE

DECAPOLIS

Ptolemais

Capernaum

Sea of Galilee

MEDITERRANEAN SEA

Nazareth

Cæsarea

SAMARIA

PEREA

Samaria

Jordan R.

ARABIA

Joppa

Jericho

Jerusalem
Bethlehem

JUDEA

The Dead Sea

Hebron

Gaza

Beersheba

SCALE OF MILES

0   5   10   20   30   40

COPYRIGHT, 1907, BY THE BIBLE STUDY PUB. CO., BOSTON.

MAP NO. 37.   ROAD MAP OF PALESTINE, OUTLINE

MAP NO. 38. ANCIENT JERUSALEM, OUTLINE

INDEX

A.

Abana, 44.
Abel Meholah, 40.
Abel Shittim, 42.
Abila, 44.
Aceldama, 22.
Adam, 40.
Admah, 41.
Adullam, Cave, 8.
Aenon, 17.
Aelia Capitolina, 25.
Ai, 19.
Aijalon, Valley, 8.
Ain Gadis, 32.
Ain Jalud, 52.
Ain Jidy, 24.
Ain Quadis, 32.
Akabah, 61.
Alexandria, 3.
Amathus, 63.
Amphipolis, 61.
Anathoth, 21.
Ancyra, 60.
Angora, 60.
Anti-Lebanon Mountains, 6, 44, 56.
Antioch in Pisidia, 60.
Antioch in Syria, xiv, 57.
Appian Way, 64.
Appii Forum, 64.
Arabah, xiv.
Arabian Desert, 1, 54.
Aram, 56.
Aram-naharaim, 55.
Argob, 46.
Ariel, 25.
Armenian Convent, 25.
Ashdod, 7.
Ashkelon, 7.
Asia Minor, 1, 5.
Asshur, 55.
Athens, xiv, 62.
Awaji, 44.

B.

Baalbec, 57.
Baal-Hazor, 15.
Baal-Zephon, 4.
Babylon, xiv, 54.
Bagdad, 54.
Banias, 34.
Barada, 44.
Beersheba, 8, 32.
Beitin, 19.
Berea, 62.
Besor, Brook, 8.

Bethany, xiv, 24.
Bethel, xiv, 12, 19.
Bethesda, 26.
Beth-horon, 32.
Bethlehem, xiv, xv, 31.
Beth-peor, 49.
Bethphage, 24.
Bethsaida Julias, 37.
Bethsaida of Galilee, 37.
Beth-Shan, xv, 40, 52, 53.
Beth-Shemesh, 8.
Bithynia, 59.
Black Sea, 1.
Blue Nile, 3.
Books, ix.
Borsippa, 55.
Bozrah, 50.
Brook Besor, 8.
Brook Cherith, 23.
Brook Jabbok, 46.
Brook Jalud, 52.
Brook Zered, 49.

C.

Cæsarea, 7.
Cæsarea Philippi, xv, 6, 34.
Calah, 55.
Calvary, 29.
Cana, xv, 10.
Canaan, 2.
Candia, 63.
Capernaum, xv, 10, 37.
Cappadocia, 59.
Carchemish, 57.
Caria, 59.
Carmel, xx, 6, 13.
Caspian Sea, 1.
Cave Adullam, 8.
Cenchreæ, 62, 63.
Central Mountain Range, 1.
Chebar, 55.
Cherith, Brook, 23.
Chinnereth, Lake, 34.
Chios, 63.
Chorazin, 37.
Church of the Holy Sepulchre, 26.
Church of St. Anne, 26.
Church of St. James, 26.
Cilicia, 59.
Citium, 63.
City of Palm Trees, 40.
Coele Syria, 56.
Colosse, 61.
Coos, 63.

Index

Corinth, xv, 62.
Crete, 63.
Cyprus, 63.

D.

Damascus, xv, 44
Damieh Ford, 40, 42.
Dan, 33.
Dead Sea Region, xv, 35, 42.
Derbe, 60.
Desert of Paran, 1.
Desert of Sin, 3.
Desert of Zin, 3.
Dibon, 49.
District of Jedur, 45.
District of Hauran, 46.
Dome of the Rock, 28.
Dothan, xv, 13.
Dur-sharrukin, 56.

E.

Eastern Mountains in Gilead, 1.
Eastern Road, 30.
Ebal, 13.
Edessa, 55.
Edom, 49.
Edrei, 46.
Egypt, xvi, 1, 3, 5.
Ekron, 7.
Elah, 8. 31.
Elim, 4.
El Lisan, 42.
El Khuds esh-Sherif, 25.
Emmaus, xvi, 31.
Endor, 9, 53.
En-gedi, 24.
En Rogel, 29.
Ephesus, 60.
Ephraim, N. T., 19.
Ephraim, O. T., 12, 47.
Ephrath, 31.
Ephron, 19.
Esdraelon, xvi, 52.
Etham, 4.
Euphrates, 1, 54.

F.

Fair Havens, 63.
Farah, 17.
Field of Blood, 22.
Fords of the Jordan, 39.
Fountain of Banias, 34.
Fountain of Gideon, 52.
Fountain of Hasbany, 33.
Fountain of Jezreel, 52.
Fountain of Siloam, 29.
Fountain of the Virgin, 29.

G.

Gadara, 47.
Galatia, 59, 60.
Galilee, xvi, 34, 36.
Garda, 47.

Garden of Gethsemane, 22.
Gath, 7.
Gaza, xvi, 7.
Geba, 20.
Gehenna, 22, 29.
Gennesaret, 36.
Gerasa, 48.
Gergesa, 38.
Gerizim, xx, 13.
Gersa, 38.
Geshur, 45.
Gethsemane, 22.
Gezer, 8.
Ghor, 39.
Gibeah of Benjamin, 20.
Gibeon, 20, 32.
Gideon, 52.
Gilboa, xx, 9, 13.
Gilead, 1, 2.
Gilgal, Samuel, 16, 17.
Gilgal, Passover, 41.
Gihon, 25, 29.
Gomorrah, 41.
Gophna, 19.
Goshen, 3.
Governor's Palace, 26.
Gulf of Akabah, 1.
Gulf of Persia, 56.
Gulf of Suez, 1.

H.

Hadad Rimmon, 52.
Hai, 19.
Hamath, 57.
Haran, xvi, 55.
Hasbany, 33.
Hasbeiya, 33.
Hauran, District of, 46.
Hazazon of the Palm, 24.
Hazazon-tamar, 24.
Hazor, 10.
Hebron, xvi, 31.
Heliopolis, Egypt, 3.
Heliopolis, Greece, 57.
Hermon, Mount, xx, 6, 34.
Hermon, Little, 9, 53.
Heshbon, 49.
Hezekiah, 26.
Hieromax, 46.
Hill of Evil Counsel, 22.
Hill of Moreh, 9, 53.
Hill of Orphel, 28.
Hinnom, 22, 25.
Hollow Syria, 56.
Holy Sepulchre, 25.
Hor, Mount, xx, 32, 50.
Huleh, 9, 34, 35.

I.

Iconium, 60.
Idumea, 49.
Italy, xvi, 5.

Index

J.

Jabbok, Brook, xvi, 39, 46.
Jabesh-Gilead, 47.
Jacob's Well, 15.
Jaffa, xvi, 7.
Jalud, Brook, 52.
Jarmuk, 46.
Jaulan, 45.
Jeba, 20.
Jebel Jermuk, 10.
Jebel Musa, 3.
Jebel Osha, 47.
Jebus, 25.
Jebus-shalem, 25.
Jedur, District of, 45.
Jehoshaphat, 22, 25.
Jeresh, xvii.
Jericho, Modern, xvii, 41.
Jericho, N. T., 40.
Jericho, O. T., 40.
Jericho, Plain of, 35.
Jerusalem, xvii, xviii, xix, 22, 24, 25.
Jeru-shalaim, 25.
Jeshimon, 23.
Jewish Quarter, 28.
Jezreel, xix, 52.
Job's Country, 46.
Joppa, xvi, 7.
Jordan Valley, xix.
Jordan, 1, 33, 39.
Joseph's Tomb, 15.
Judah, 23.

K.

Kadesh-Barnea, 32.
Kedar, 54.
Kedesh, 9.
Kenath, 46.
Khersa, 38.
Kidron, 23.
Kingdom of the Ammonites, 47.
Kingdom of Antiochus, 59.
Kingdom of Geshur, 45.
Kingdom of Og, 46.
Kirjath-jearim, 31.
Kir of Moab, 49.
Kishon, 6.
Kurun Hattin, 10.

L.

Laish, 34.
Lake Chinnereth, 34.
Lake of Galilee, 34.
Lake Huleh, 9, 34, 35.
Lake Merom, 9.
Lake of Tiberias, 34.
Lake Urumiah, 56.
Lake Van, 54.
Land of Goshen, 3.
Land of the Hebrews, 2.

Land of Israel, 2.
Land of Kedar, 54.
Land of Moab, 48.
Land of Promise, 2.
Land of the Twin Rivers. 54.
Land of Uz, 46, 54.
Lantern Slides, xxi.
Laodicaea, 61.
Lebanon, xix, 2.
Lebanon Mountains, 6, 56.
Lechaeum, 62.
Lejah, 46.
Lejjun, 52.
Leontes River, 6, 9.
Lesbos, 63.
Liddan, 33.
Litany, River, 6.
Little Hermon, 9, 53.
Lod, 7.
Lower Egypt, 3.
Lower Gihon, 29.
Lower Ford, 42.
Lud, 7.
Lycaonia, 60.
Lydda, xix, 7.
Lycia, 59.
Lydia, 59.
Lystra, 60.

M.

Machaerus, xix.
Madai, 56.
Magdala, xix, 36.
Mahanaim, 47.
Malta, 63.
Mamre, 31.
Manual Work.
Maps.
Marah, 4.
Maritime Plain, 1.
Mar-Saba, xix.
Masada, 24.
Medeba, 49.
Media, 1.
Mediterranean Sea, 1.
Megiddo, 51, 52.
Mejdel, 37.
Melita, 63.
Merom, Lake, 9, 35.
Mesopotamia, 1, 5, 54.
Michmash, 19.
Migdol, 37.
Miletus, 60.
Mitylene, 63.
Mizpah, xix, 21, 32. 48.
Moab, 42, 48.
Monastery of Mar Saba, 24.
Moreh, 9, 51, 53.
Moriah, 28.
Mount of Beatitudes, xix, 10.
Mount Carmel, xx, 6, 13.
Mount Ebal, 13.
Mount Ephraim, 12.

Mount Gerizim, xx, 13.
Mount Gilboa, xx, 13, 53.
Mount Hermon, xx, 6, 34.
Mount Hor, xx, 32, 50.
Mount Jebel Jermuk, 10.
Mount Lebanon, 2.
Mount Moriah, 28.
Mount Moreh, 51.
Mount Nebo, xx.
Mount of Olives, 22, 30.
Mount Pisgah, 47.
Mount of Samaria, 15.
Mount Seir, 49.
Mount Sinai, 3.
Mount Tabor, xx, 9, 53.
Mount of Temptation, 31.
Mount of the Transfiguration of Christ, 6.
Mount Zion, 25.
Mountains of Anti-Lebanon, 6, 44, 56.
Mugheir, 55.
Mukmas, 19.
Myra, 60.

N.

Nablous, 14.
Nazareth, xx, 10.
Nain, xx, 10, 53.
Neapolis, O. T., 14.
Neapolis, N. T., 61.
Nebo, xx.
Negeb, 32.
Nifur, 55.
Nile, 1, 3.
Nimrim Ford, 42.
Nimrud, 55.
Nineveh, 55.
Nippur, 55.
Nob, 21.
Nobah, 46.
Northern Egypt, 3.
Northern Road, 30.
Northwestern Road, 32.

O.

Og, 46.
Ophni, 19.
Orfa, 55.
Ophel, 28.
Ophrah, 19.

P.

Palace of Herod, 25.
Palestine, xiv, 1, 2, 5.
Palmyra, 57.
Pamphylia, 59.
Paneas, 34.
Paphlagonia, 59.
Paphos, 63.
Paran, 1, 3.
Patmos, 63.

Pella, 47.
Peniel, 48.
Penuel, 48.
Perea, 47.
Pergamos, 61.
Persian Gulf, 1, 56.
Persepolis, 56.
Petra, xx, 50.
Pharpar, 44.
Philadelphia, 48, 61.
Philippi, 61.
Phrygia, 59, 60.
Pictures, xiii-xxi.
Pihahiroth, 4.
Pisgah, 47.
Pisidia, 60.
Plain of Abel Shittim, 42.
Plain of Esdraelon, 52.
Plain of Gennesaret, 36.
Plain of Jericho, 35.
Plain of Mamre, 31.
Plain of Moab, 42.
Plain of Rephaim, 30.
Plain of Sharon, 7.
Pontus, 59.
Pool of Bethesda, 26.
Pool of Gibeon, 20.
Pool of Hezekiah, 26.
Pool of Samaria, 16.
Pool of Siloam, 29.
Potter's Field, 22.
Pozzuoli, 64.
Ptolemais, 7.
Puteoli, 64.

R.

Rabbath-Ammon, 48.
Rachel's Tomb, 31.
Ramah, xx.
Ramah of Benjamin, 20.
Rameses, 4.
Ramleh, xx.
Ramoth-Gilead, 48.
Ras es Sufsafeh, 4.
Reference Books, ix.
Region of the Dead Sea, xv.
Rephaim, 30.
Rephidim, 4.
Rheggio, 64.
Rhegium, 64.
Rhodes, 63.
River Abana, 44.
River Awaji, 44.
River Barada, 44.
River Chebar, 55.
River Euphrates, 1, 54.
River Farah, 17.
River Jabbok, 39.
River Jordan, 1, 33.
River Kishon, 6.
River Litany, 6.
River Nile, 1.
River Pharpar, 44.

Index

Riblah, 57.
River Tigris, 1, 5, 54.
River Xanthus, 60.
River Yarmuk, 39.
Robinson's Arch, 28.
Rock Rimmon, 19.
Roman Empire, 1.
Rome, xx, xxi, 64.
Royal Quarries, 27.

S.

Salamis, 63.
Salem, 25.
Saloniki, 62.
Samaria, Hill of, 15.
Samaria, Modern, xxi, 13.
Samaria, N. T., 12.
Samaria, O. T., 12.
Samaria, Pool of, 16.
Samos, 63.
Samothracia, 63.
Sardis, 61.
Scythopolis, 52.
Sea of Galilee, 36.
Sebaste, 16.
Seilun, 16. .
Seir, 49.
Selah, 50.
Seleucia, 57.
Sharon, 7.
Shechem, xxi, 13.
Shephelah, 8.
Shiloh, xxi, 16.
Shinar, 54.
Shunem, 10, 52.
Shur, 3.
Shushan, 56.
Sidon, xxi, 6.
Siloam, 29.
Sin, 3.
Sinai, 3.
Sinai Peninsula, 1, 3.
Six Zones, 5.
Slides, xxi.
Sodom, 41.
Sorek, 8.
Southern Desert, 2.
Southen Egypt, 3.
Southern Road, 30.
South Galatia, 60.
Southwestern Road, 31.
Spring of Gideon, 52.
Stanchio, 63.
St. Paul's Port, 63.
St. Stephen's Gate, 26.
Stereopticon Slides, xxi.
Succoth, 4, 40.
Suez, 1.
Suf, 48.
Supplies, ix.
Susa, 56.
Sychar, 14.
Syracuse, 64.
Syria, 1, 55.

T.

Taanach, 52.
Tabor, xx, 9, 53.
Tadnor, 57.
Tarsus, 60.
Tekoa, 24.
Thebes, 3.
The Holy City, 25.
The Holy Land, 3.
Thessalonica, xxi, 62.
Three Taverns, 64.
Threshing Floor of Araunah, 28.
Thyatira, 61.
Tiberias, xxi, 34, 36.
Tigris, 1, 5, 54.
Timnath, 8.
Tirzah, 15.
Tophet, 22, 29.
Trachonitis, 46.
Troas, 61.
Trogyllium, 63.
Twin Rivers, 54.
Tyre, xxi, 6.
Tyropoeon, 25.

U.

Um-Keis, 47.
Upper Egypt, 3.
Upper Gihon, 29.
Ur of Chaldees, 55.
Urumiah, 56.
Uz, 46, 54.

V.

Vale of Hebron, 31.
Valley of Aijalon, 8.
Valley of Dothan, 13.
Valley of Elah, 8, 31.
Valley of Gihon, 25.
Valley of Hinnom, 22, 25.
Valley of Jehoshaphat, 22, 25.
Valley of Jezreel, 52.
Valley of the Jordan, 39.
Valley of Megiddo, 51.
Valley of Shechem, 13.
Valley of the Sorek, 8.
Van, 54.
Via Dolorosa, 26.
Village of Siloam, 29.

W.

Wailing Place of the Jews, 28.
Watch-tower, 37.
Waters of Merom, 34, 35.
Western Road, 31.
White Nile, 3.
Wilderness of Judah, 23.
Wilderness of Mount Sinai, 3.
Wilderness of Paran, 3.
Wilderness of Shur, 3.
Wilderness of Sin, 3.
Wilderness of Zin, 3.
Wood of Ephraim, 47.

Index

X.

Xanthus, 60.

Y.

Yarmuk, 39.

Z.

Zagros Mountains. 1. 56.

Zaretan, 40.
Zeboim, 41.
Zered, Brook, 49.
Zerin, 15, 52.
Zin, 3.
Zion, 25.
Ziz, 24.
Zoar, 41.
Zor, 39.
Zorah, 8.